BASIC BIBLE   OF THE
DOCTRINES   CHRISTIAN FAITH

EXPLAINING THE DOCTRINE OF SALVATION

Edward D. Andrews

EXPLAINING THE DOCTRINE OF SALVATION

Basic Bible Doctrines of the Christian Faith

Edward D. Andrews

Christian Publishing House

Cambridge, Ohio

CHRISTIAN PUBLISHING HOUSE

FOUNDED 2005

THE GREEK-ENGLISH NEW TESTAMENT INTERLINEAR: With a Textual Commentary On The Greek New Testament by Edward D. Andrews

ISBN-10: 0692634495

ISBN-13: 978-0692634493

Table of Contents

Book Description

"EXPLAINING THE DOCTRINE OF SALVATION: Basic Bible Doctrines of the Christian Faith" is a comprehensive and thought-provoking exploration of the multifaceted concept of salvation from a Christian perspective. Authored by a renowned conservative Bible scholar, this book delves into the depths of Biblical teachings, offering a detailed examination of salvation's various aspects as portrayed in the scriptures. The book is a compelling resource for theologians, pastors, students of theology, and any Christian seeking a deeper understanding of their faith.

Key Features:

- **In-Depth Biblical Analysis**: Each chapter methodically examines key Biblical narratives—from Noah's Ark to the Babylonian Exile—highlighting their significance in the broader context of salvation.

- **Critical Examination of Calvinism:** The appendices provide a thorough critique of Calvinist doctrines such as Total Depravity and Unconditional Election, presenting scriptural counterarguments for a more balanced view of salvation.

- **Focus on Enduring Faith and Repentance**: The book emphasizes the necessity of ongoing faith, challenging the notion of 'Once Saved, Always Saved' and advocating for a dynamic understanding of Christian perseverance.

- **Balanced Theological Perspective**: While critiquing certain doctrinal viewpoints, the book maintains a respectful approach, fostering a nuanced understanding of complex theological issues.

- **Accessible to a Broad Audience**: Written in clear, comprehensible language, the book addresses both the scholarly community and lay Christians, making complex theological concepts accessible to all.

Audience Appeal:

"EXPLAINING THE DOCTRINE OF SALVATION" is particularly suited for readers interested in Biblical studies, Christian theology, and church history. Its thorough analysis makes it an invaluable resource for theological students, educators, clergy, and laypersons desiring a deeper understanding of Christian salvation doctrines.

Overall, this book offers a rich, scripturally grounded exploration of salvation, challenging traditional views while encouraging readers to engage deeply with Biblical teachings. It's an essential addition to any theological library, promising to enlighten, educate, and inspire its readers.

Edward D. Andrews

Preface

In "EXPLAINING THE DOCTRINE OF SALVATION: Basic Bible Doctrines of the Christian Faith," we embark on a journey through the vast and profound landscape of Christian salvation. This book is born out of a deep desire to elucidate one of the most fundamental yet complex doctrines of Christian theology. It is an endeavor to bridge the gap between scholarly theological discussion and the practical understanding needed by believers in their daily walk of faith.

The inspiration for this work stems from a growing concern over the oversimplification of salvation in contemporary Christian thought and the need to address common misconceptions, particularly those associated with Calvinistic doctrines. The aim is not to dispute for the sake of argument but to foster a richer, more nuanced understanding of salvation that is firmly rooted in Biblical scripture.

Each chapter in this book is crafted to explore different Biblical narratives and themes, unraveling the multifaceted nature of salvation. From the ancient story of Noah to the liberation from Babylonian captivity, these narratives are not just historical accounts but are deeply emblematic of God's plan of salvation for humanity. They serve as a lens through which we can understand the broader redemptive work of God through time.

The appendices address specific Calvinist doctrines, offering a critical yet respectful analysis. This examination is essential, not only for theological clarity but also for helping believers understand the implications of these doctrines on their perception of God and their own spiritual journey.

As you delve into this book, whether you are a theologian, pastor, student, or a layperson seeking to deepen your faith, my hope is that it will challenge you to reflect, question, and grow. This work is an invitation to engage with the Biblical texts, to wrestle with difficult questions, and to embrace the richness of God's salvation story.

It is my prayer that this book will serve as a valuable resource in your spiritual and intellectual journey, enriching your understanding of what it means to be saved and how this profound truth impacts every aspect of Christian life.

Edward D. Andrews

Author of 220+ books and Chief Translator for the Updated American Standard Version (UASV)

Introduction

In the quest to understand the Christian faith, the doctrine of salvation stands as a pivotal concept that has engaged theologians, pastors, and believers throughout the ages. The nature of salvation—what it means, how it is obtained, and its implications for life—remains a subject of vital importance and, at times, intense debate within the Christian community. This book, "EXPLAINING THE DOCTRINE OF SALVATION: Basic Bible Doctrines of the Christian Faith," is a journey into the heart of these discussions, offering a comprehensive exploration of salvation as presented in the Bible.

In the pages that follow, we will traverse through key Biblical narratives, each shedding light on different aspects of salvation. From the ancient story of Noah and the Great Flood to the liberation of the Israelites from Egyptian bondage, these stories are not merely historical accounts but are rich with theological significance. They offer insights into the nature of God, His interaction with humanity, and His overarching plan for redemption.

Moreover, this book critically examines various doctrines that have shaped Christian thought, particularly those within Calvinism. It is important to note that this critique is not intended to diminish the contributions of these theological traditions but to engage with them meaningfully, understanding their nuances and the scriptural basis upon which they stand.

Salvation is more than a theological concept; it is a reality that touches every aspect of human existence. It is about the transformation of lives, the restoration of broken relationships, and the hope of eternity. It is also about the here and now—how we understand our place in the world, our purpose, and how we relate to God and to one another.

As we embark on this exploration, the goal is to foster a deeper appreciation for the rich tapestry of Biblical teachings on salvation. This book aims to challenge, inform, and inspire you to delve deeper into your own understanding of these truths. Whether you are a seasoned theologian or someone just beginning your journey of faith, it is my hope that these pages will be a valuable resource in your spiritual and intellectual journey.

Through this exploration, may we come to a fuller understanding of what it means to be saved, the incredible grace that underlies this gift, and the responsibility it places upon us as recipients of such unmerited favor. Let us begin this journey together, with open hearts and minds, ready to discover the profound truths of salvation as revealed in the scriptures.

CHAPTER 1 Salvation Amidst a Corrupt World: Noah's Ark and the Great Flood

The Wickedness of the Antediluvian World

The Spiritual Rebellion and its Earthly Impact

In the antediluvian period, the world witnessed a profound spiritual rebellion that had significant earthly consequences. The book of Genesis describes a time when "the sons of the true God" began to notice and take as wives the daughters of men (Genesis 6:1-2). This phrase "sons of the true God" is understood to refer to angelic beings, a view corroborated by similar terminology used in Job 1:6. The actions of these angels were in direct violation of the boundaries set by Jehovah for the spiritual and human realms.

Genesis 6: The Nephilim and the Corruption of Humanity

The result of these unnatural unions were the Nephilim, a hybrid offspring described as "the mighty ones who were of old, the men of fame" (Genesis 6:4). The Hebrew term "Nephilim" is derived from the root 'npl,' meaning 'to fall,' indicating their role as "Fellers" or those who cause others to fall. This description aligns with the characterization of the Nephilim as giants and as vicious bullies, contributing significantly to the moral decay and violence of that era.

The Role of the Nephilim in the Antediluvian Corruption

The presence of the Nephilim exacerbated the wickedness on earth. Their formidable size and strength, coupled with their corrupt nature, likely played a central role in the intensification of violence and immorality that pervaded the pre-Flood world. The Bible's depiction of this period is one of widespread corruption and violence, where "every inclination of the thoughts of the human heart was only evil all the time" (Genesis 6:5).

Divine Judgment and the Preservation of Righteousness

Jehovah's response to the rampant wickedness was the decree of the Great Flood, a divine judgment intended to cleanse the earth. Noah, a righteous man in the eyes of God, was chosen to preserve the human race and the animal kinds through the building of the ark (Genesis 6:9-22). The Flood thus represents God's commitment to righteousness and His rejection of the corruption that had overtaken humanity.

The Fate of the Rebel Angels and the Nephilim

As the Flood waters prevailed upon the earth, the Nephilim and their human mothers perished. The rebel angels who had materialized human bodies to engage in these forbidden unions were forced to dematerialize and return to the spirit realm. However, they could not resume their original position with God. Instead, as stated in Jude 6 and 2 Peter 2:4, they were consigned to "dense [spiritual] darkness," or Tartarus, a state of disgrace and restraint awaiting final judgment. This action by Jehovah effectively severed these fallen angels from their former estate, leaving them as demons, the spiritual companions of Satan, furthering his rebellion and wicked purposes.

Lessons from Antediluvian Times

The account of the antediluvian world offers profound insights into the nature of divine judgment, the importance of maintaining the sanctity of the created order, and the consequences of spiritual rebellion. It underscores Jehovah's commitment to righteousness and justice, even as it highlights His provision for salvation and preservation of the righteous, exemplified in the story of Noah. This narrative sets a precedent for understanding the gravity of sin, the reality of divine judgment, and the necessity of adhering to God's standards of righteousness.

The Construction of the Ark: A Beacon of Hope

Divine Command and Noah's Obedience

The construction of the Ark was initiated by a direct command from Jehovah to Noah, found in Genesis 6:14-16. This command was not merely a call to build a vessel, but a divine directive for preserving life amidst impending judgment. Noah's response was one of unquestioning obedience, a testament to his faith and righteousness. In Hebrews 11:7, Noah's action is described as an act of faith, a tangible response to a warning about things not yet seen.

Technical Specifications and Symbolism

The Ark's dimensions and design, detailed in Genesis, are of great significance. Measuring approximately 450 feet in length, 75 feet in width, and 45 feet in height, the Ark was a massive structure for its time. Its three decks, a door on its side, and a roof with an opening for ventilation were designed for the dual purpose of survival and functionality. The use of gopher wood, a term unique in the Hebrew Scriptures, along with pitch for waterproofing, underscores the meticulous care in its construction. Symbolically, the Ark represented Jehovah's provision for salvation, a refuge from divine judgment.

The Ark as a Prefiguration of Christ's Salvation

The Ark is often seen as a type, or a prefiguration, of the salvation offered through Jesus Christ. Just as the Ark was the only means of physical salvation from the Flood,

Christ is portrayed in the New Testament as the sole means of spiritual salvation (John 14:6; Acts 4:12). The Apostle Peter makes a direct connection between the Ark and baptism, which now saves Christians, not by removing dirt from the flesh, but as an appeal to God for a good conscience through the resurrection of Jesus Christ (1 Peter 3:20-21).

The Construction Process: A Testimony of Faith

The construction of the Ark was a monumental task, likely spanning several decades. This prolonged period of building was not just a physical undertaking but also a spiritual and moral proclamation. 2 Peter 2:5 refers to Noah as a "preacher of righteousness," suggesting that the construction of the Ark was a testimony to the surrounding people, an implicit warning of the coming judgment and a call to repentance.

The Ark's Role in God's Salvific Plan

The Ark was central to God's plan of salvation during the Flood. It was not merely an escape from physical destruction but also a means to preserve the human race and animal kinds, ensuring the continuation of God's creation post-Flood. The salvation of Noah and his family, eight souls in total, through the Ark signified the preservation of a righteous lineage through which God's redemptive plan for humanity would continue to unfold.

The Enduring Legacy of the Ark

The story of the Ark's construction and its role in the Great Flood stands as a powerful narrative of divine salvation amidst a corrupt world. It serves as a testament to the sovereignty of Jehovah, His judgment against wickedness, and His mercy in providing a means of salvation. The Ark's enduring legacy is a reminder of the importance of faith, obedience, and hope in the face of judgment, characteristics that are essential for understanding the broader biblical theme of salvation.

Noah's Faith and Obedience

Noah's Righteousness in a Wicked World

Noah's life stood in stark contrast to the pervasive wickedness of his time. The Genesis narrative describes the world as corrupt and filled with violence (Genesis 6:11-12), yet Noah is singled out as a righteous man, blameless among the people of his time (Genesis 6:9). His righteousness was not just a moral standing; it was a demonstration of his unswerving faith in Jehovah.

The Nature of Noah's Faith

Hebrews 11:7 highlights the essence of Noah's faith: "By faith Noah, being warned by God concerning events as yet unseen, in reverent fear constructed an ark for the saving of his household." This verse captures the substance of faith as described in Hebrews 11:1 – "the assurance of things hoped for, the conviction of things not seen." Noah's faith was not a passive belief but an active trust in God's word and promises.

Obedience Amidst Unseen Realities

Noah's obedience was remarkable because it was based on things not yet seen. The concept of a global flood was unprecedented, and the act of building an ark was a monumental task that required unwavering commitment. Noah's obedience, as a response to God's warning, was a testament to his faith. His actions were not based on visible evidence but on his trust in God's word.

The Prophetic Role of Noah

Noah's construction of the Ark served a prophetic role, symbolizing both judgment and salvation. 2 Peter 2:5 describes Noah as a "preacher of righteousness," suggesting that his life and actions served as a divine message to his contemporaries. The very act of building the Ark was a testimony to the impending judgment and an implicit invitation to repentance.

Endurance in the Midst of Mockery

Building the Ark likely subjected Noah and his family to mockery and scorn from their contemporaries. The prolonged nature of the construction, combined with the lack of immediate evidence of a flood, would have made Noah's task seem foolish in the eyes of others. Nevertheless, Noah's endurance in the face of ridicule further underscores the depth of his faith and obedience.

Theological Implications of Noah's Faith

Noah's faith and obedience provide profound theological insights. First, they illustrate the principle that true faith results in action. James 2:26 echoes this sentiment, stating that "faith apart from works is dead." Second, Noah's life serves as an example of living righteously in a corrupt society. His faithfulness amidst widespread wickedness offers a model for believers in every generation.

Salvation Through Judgment

The Ark was a means of salvation through judgment. Noah's entrance into the Ark symbolized God's provision of salvation for those who trust in Him. Just as the Ark shielded Noah from the waters of judgment, so does faith in Christ protect believers from eternal condemnation (Romans 8:1).

Noah's Legacy: A Foreshadowing of Christ

Noah's faith and obedience prefigured the coming of Christ. Just as Noah acted on God's word to bring salvation to his household, Christ obeyed the Father to bring salvation to humanity. Furthermore, as Noah mediated physical salvation through the Ark, Jesus mediates eternal salvation through His sacrificial death and resurrection (1 Timothy 2:5-6).

The Enduring Message of Noah's Faith

Noah's faith and obedience amidst a corrupt world continue to resonate with profound significance for believers today. They teach the value of steadfast faith in God's promises, the importance of obedience even when facing unseen realities, and the assurance of God's deliverance through judgment. Noah's life, therefore, stands as an enduring testament to the power of faith and the certainty of God's salvation plan.

The Cataclysmic Flood: Eradication of Evil

The Divine Decision for a Global Flood

The decision by Jehovah to bring a global flood, as described in Genesis 6:7, was a response to the pervasive wickedness and corruption that had consumed humanity. The world had reached a state of moral depravity, where "every intention of the thoughts of [man's] heart was only evil continually" (Genesis 6:5). This profound statement of human wickedness underscores the necessity of divine intervention.

The Scope and Nature of the Flood

The Flood was not a local or regional event, but a cataclysmic, global deluge that reshaped the earth's landscape. Genesis 7:19-20 describes the waters prevailing "exceedingly upon the earth," covering even the highest mountains. This universal scope emphasizes the extent of God's judgment against sin and the thoroughness of the eradication of evil.

The Flood as an Act of Divine Justice

The Flood stands as a divine act of justice, eliminating the widespread wickedness that had defined antediluvian society. This judgment was directed not only against humanity but also against the corrupted creation, which included the Nephilim and the tainted animal life (Genesis 6:11-13). The Flood was a necessary and righteous response to sin, affirming God's holiness and intolerance of evil.

Salvation and Judgment Intertwined

In the midst of judgment, the narrative of the Flood intertwines themes of salvation. Noah and his family, eight persons in total, were saved because of Noah's righteousness (Genesis 7:1). The Ark, as a means of salvation, highlights the principle that while God is just in His judgment, He is also merciful in providing a way of escape for the righteous.

The Covenantal Significance of the Flood

The Flood marked a turning point in God's covenantal relationship with humanity. After the waters receded, God established a covenant with Noah and his descendants, promising never to destroy the earth again with a flood (Genesis 9:11). The rainbow, set as a sign of this covenant (Genesis 9:13), symbolizes God's grace and faithfulness.

Theological Implications of the Flood

Theologically, the Flood narrative addresses several key concepts:

- The seriousness of sin and its consequences.

- The doctrine of divine judgment and wrath against unrighteousness.

- The mercy and grace of God in preserving a remnant.

- The concept of a new beginning post-judgment, as seen in the renewal of the earth and the re-establishment of human society under Noah's lineage.

The Flood in New Testament Theology

In the New Testament, the Flood is referenced as a typological event foreshadowing the final judgment. Jesus Christ Himself likened the days of Noah to the days of the Son of Man (Luke 17:26-27). Similarly, the apostles Peter and Paul used the Flood as an example of God's judgment against ungodliness and His salvation for the righteous (2 Peter 2:5, 3:5-6; 1 Peter 3:20).

The Flood as a Paradigm of Future Judgment and Salvation

The narrative of the Flood serves as a paradigm for understanding future divine judgment and salvation. Just as the Flood brought judgment upon a corrupt world while providing salvation through the Ark, so will the final judgment bring condemnation to the unrighteous and deliverance to those who are in Christ.

The Enduring Message of the Flood

The Flood narrative is a powerful testimony to the holiness and justice of God, as well as His mercy and grace. It serves as a sober reminder of the consequences of sin, the certainty of divine judgment, and the availability of salvation to those who are righteous. The story of Noah and the Flood continues to resonate as a profound example of God's redemptive plan in action, affirming the themes of judgment, salvation, and new beginnings that are central to the Christian faith.

A New Beginning: God's Covenant with Noah

The Covenant's Establishment

The covenant established by God with Noah following the Flood represents a pivotal moment in biblical history. This covenant, detailed in Genesis 9:8-17, signifies God's promise not only to Noah but to all living creatures and the earth itself. It was a binding agreement, a solemn promise that God would never again destroy all flesh with a flood (Genesis 9:11). This covenant, characterized by its unilateral nature, where God alone makes and upholds the promise, underscores His grace and faithfulness.

The Universal Scope of the Covenant

Unlike future covenants made with specific individuals or the nation of Israel, the Noahic covenant was universal in its scope. It extended to every living creature and all successive generations, establishing a fundamental relationship between God and all of creation. This universality reflects the broad reach of God's mercy and the intrinsic value He places on His creation.

The Rainbow: A Sign of the Covenant

God designated the rainbow as the sign of this covenant (Genesis 9:13). The appearance of the rainbow in the clouds serves as a visual reminder of God's enduring promise. This natural phenomenon, which occurs when sunlight and water droplets combine to produce a spectrum of light in the sky, is a symbol of hope and God's faithfulness. The rainbow's emergence after rain serves as a reminder of God's mercy prevailing over judgment.

Theological Implications of the Covenant

The Noahic covenant holds several theological implications:

1. The Sanctity of Life: Following the Flood, God establishes the sanctity of human life, emphasizing that human beings are made in His image and that the taking of human life demands accountability (Genesis 9:5-6).

2. The Continuity of Creation: The covenant assures the regularity and continuity of the natural world (Genesis 8:22). This assurance is foundational to human existence and the predictability of the seasons, which are crucial for survival and cultivation.

3. The Grace of God: The covenant demonstrates God's grace in offering a new beginning to humanity despite the pervasive sinfulness that led to the Flood. It reflects God's patience and His desire for restoration and reconciliation.

Post-Flood Regulations

Alongside the covenant, God provides Noah and his descendants with specific instructions and regulations. These include the sanctity of blood (Genesis 9:4) and the establishment of capital punishment for murder (Genesis 9:6). These regulations set forth the principles of justice and the value of life, laying the foundation for human society and governance.

Noah's Covenant in Relation to Subsequent Covenants

The Noahic covenant serves as a backdrop against which subsequent biblical covenants are understood. It is a covenant of preservation, ensuring the stability of the earth as the stage upon which the drama of redemption, culminating in the New Covenant through Jesus Christ, unfolds. This covenant, therefore, establishes the basic conditions necessary for God's redemptive plan to proceed throughout human history.

The Covenant and Christian Theology

In Christian theology, the Noahic covenant is seen as an early expression of God's redemptive purposes. It sets the stage for the later covenants with Abraham, Moses, and ultimately the New Covenant in Christ. This progression from a universal covenant with all creation to a specific covenant with a chosen people, and finally to a new covenant for all humanity, demonstrates the unfolding of God's salvific plan.

Conclusion: The Enduring Legacy of the Noahic Covenant

The Noahic covenant stands as a testament to God's commitment to His creation and His unwavering faithfulness. It is a covenant that speaks of new beginnings, hope, and the assurance of God's grace and mercy. The legacy of this covenant is seen in its continual reminder of God's promise, echoed every time a rainbow appears in the sky, assuring us of God's perpetual care and the enduring nature of His promises.

Edward D. Andrews

CHAPTER 2: From Slavery to Royalty: The Salvation of Joseph

Joseph's Early Life and Trials

Introduction to Joseph's Early Life

Joseph's life, a remarkable narrative of divine providence and human resilience, begins in the context of a complex family dynamic. Born to Jacob, later named Israel, and his beloved wife Rachel, Joseph was the eleventh of twelve sons. His early life, as recorded in Genesis 37, was marked by favoritism and familial discord, factors that played a crucial role in the unfolding of his life's journey.

Favoritism and the Coat of Many Colors

Joseph's status as the favored son of Jacob is exemplified by the gift of a coat of many colors (Genesis 37:3). This coat, a symbol of favor and possibly of future leadership, incited jealousy and resentment among his brothers. The preferential treatment accorded to Joseph by Jacob created a rift within the family, setting the stage for the trials Joseph would face.

Dreams of Destiny and Their Consequences

Joseph's life took a dramatic turn when he shared two significant dreams with his family (Genesis 37:5-11). In these dreams, symbols of sheaves of grain and celestial bodies bowing to Joseph suggested his future rise to a position of authority and dominance. While these dreams were prophetic and divinely inspired, their sharing exacerbated the existing tensions, leading his brothers to conspire against him.

Betrayal and Sold into Slavery

Joseph's trials intensified when his brothers, driven by envy, betrayed him. Initially plotting to kill him, they eventually settled on selling him into slavery to a caravan of Ishmaelites traveling to Egypt (Genesis 37:28). This act of betrayal by his own brothers was the beginning of Joseph's journey from favored son to a slave in a foreign land.

Joseph in Potiphar's House

Joseph's time in Egypt began in the household of Potiphar, an officer of Pharaoh (Genesis 39:1-6). Despite his circumstances, Joseph excelled, earning Potiphar's trust and becoming overseer of his house. This period of Joseph's life highlighted his exceptional character and God's favor, even in the midst of trials. It also set the stage for subsequent events that would lead to his imprisonment.

False Accusations and Imprisonment

Joseph faced a significant trial when falsely accused of misconduct by Potiphar's wife (Genesis 39:7-20). Despite his innocence and integrity, he was imprisoned, a victim of injustice. Joseph's experience in prison, however, was not devoid of God's presence. The Lord was with him, granting him favor and success even within the confines of the jail (Genesis 39:21-23).

Joseph's Faith and Character

Throughout these early trials, Joseph's character remained steadfast. He demonstrated resilience, integrity, and faith in God. His ability to thrive in adverse situations, whether in Potiphar's house or in prison, speaks to his trust in God's sovereignty and his capacity to find strength in his faith.

Divine Providence in Joseph's Trials

The trials of Joseph's early life, while challenging, were part of a larger divine plan. Each event, from his betrayal to his false imprisonment, was instrumental in positioning Joseph for the role he would later play in Egypt. These experiences, though painful, were integral to the fulfillment of the dreams he had as a youth and to the salvation he would eventually bring to his family and many others.

The Significance of Joseph's Early Life

Joseph's early life and trials illustrate critical themes in the doctrine of salvation. They underscore the role of divine providence in human affairs, the importance of faith and integrity in the face of adversity, and the mysterious ways in which God can use even unjust circumstances to bring about His purposes. Joseph's story is a powerful testament to the truth that God's plans are ultimately for good, even when they involve periods of hardship and testing.

From the Pit to Potiphar's House

The Betrayal and Sale into Slavery

Joseph's descent from a beloved son to a slave begins with a profound act of betrayal by his own brothers. Motivated by envy and resentment, they seize him and cast him into a pit, intending to leave him to die (Genesis 37:18-24). This act is a vivid portrayal of the degradation of familial bonds under the weight of jealousy and hatred. However, instead of leaving him to perish, they decide to profit from their treachery by selling Joseph to a caravan of Ishmaelites headed to Egypt (Genesis 37:28). This sale marks a critical turning point in Joseph's life, as he is forcibly taken away from his homeland and family.

Providence in Joseph's Downfall

Despite the apparent misfortune, there is a clear thread of divine providence in these events. The decision to sell Joseph, rather than kill him, though motivated by greed and callousness, is instrumental in God's plan for Joseph's life and the eventual salvation of his family. It is a prime example of how God can use even the evil intentions of men to bring about His greater purposes (Genesis 50:20).

Arrival at Potiphar's House

Joseph's arrival in Egypt marks the beginning of a new chapter in his life. He is purchased by Potiphar, an officer of Pharaoh and captain of the guard (Genesis 39:1). This transition from a pit to the house of a high-ranking official in Egypt, while a significant improvement from his previous predicament, still represents a state of enslavement and vulnerability.

God's Favor in Adversity

In Potiphar's house, Joseph rises to a position of responsibility and authority. Genesis 39:2-6 describes how the Lord was with Joseph, granting him success in everything he did. This divine favor is a testament to Joseph's faithfulness and integrity. Despite his circumstances, Joseph does not waver in his commitment to God and his moral principles.

Joseph's Management and Success

Joseph's management of Potiphar's household affairs demonstrates his exceptional administrative and leadership skills. His success as a steward is so pronounced that Potiphar entrusts everything he owns into Joseph's care, a remarkable turn of events for a foreign slave. This period of Joseph's life highlights his resilience, adaptability, and unwavering faith in God.

Testing of Character

Joseph's time in Potiphar's house is also a period of character testing. His response to the advances of Potiphar's wife (Genesis 39:7-12) reflects his steadfast commitment to righteousness and his fear of God. His refusal to succumb to temptation, despite the potential benefits of compliance, is a powerful statement of his moral integrity and his trust in God's providence.

Falsely Accused and Imprisonment

Joseph's righteous stance leads to false accusation and subsequent imprisonment (Genesis 39:13-20). This injustice, a result of maintaining his integrity, seems to be a setback in his life. However, even in prison, Joseph finds favor in the eyes of the Lord and the prison warden (Genesis 39:21-23). His imprisonment, like his enslavement, is a step in the unfolding of God's plan for him.

God's Sovereignty in Joseph's Journey

The trajectory of Joseph's life from the pit to Potiphar's house and then to prison is a profound illustration of God's sovereignty. Each phase of Joseph's journey, though filled with hardship and injustice, is underpinned by God's guiding hand. These experiences, while challenging, are shaping Joseph for the significant role he is to play in Egypt and for the eventual deliverance of his family.

Conclusion: From Trials to Triumph

Joseph's journey from the pit to Potiphar's house is a narrative of faith, resilience, and divine providence. It exemplifies how God works through trials and adversity to achieve His purposes. Joseph's story is a testament to the truth that God's plans are not thwarted by human actions, no matter how malicious. Instead, God sovereignly uses such circumstances to prepare His servants for greater tasks and to bring about His salvation plan.

Unjust Imprisonment and Divine Providence

The Context of Joseph's Imprisonment

Joseph's journey from Potiphar's house to prison is marked by a grave injustice. Falsely accused by Potiphar's wife of misconduct (Genesis 39:12-19), Joseph faces the wrath of Potiphar, leading to his imprisonment. This incident, while seemingly a setback, is deeply intertwined with divine providence and the unfolding of God's salvific plan.

The Nature of Joseph's Trial

The trial Joseph faces is twofold: it is a test of his personal integrity and a challenge to his faith in God's providence. Despite his innocence, he is thrust into a situation where his moral character is put to the test. His unwavering commitment to righteousness in the face of temptation and subsequent false accusation highlights his deep-rooted faith and integrity.

Divine Providence in Joseph's Imprisonment

Joseph's imprisonment, though unjust, is not outside the realm of God's sovereignty. Throughout the biblical narrative, it becomes evident that God's hand is at work even in the darkest of circumstances (Genesis 39:21). The experiences Joseph endures in prison are instrumental in preparing him for future roles that are pivotal in the fulfillment of God's larger plan for him and his family.

Joseph in the Egyptian Prison

In the Egyptian prison, Joseph once again finds favor in the eyes of the Lord and the prison warden (Genesis 39:21-23). His ability to gain trust and responsibility, even in confinement, speaks to his exceptional character and God's favor upon him. This period is significant not only for Joseph's personal growth but also for the relationships and opportunities that arise within the prison walls.

Interpreting Dreams: A Gift from God

Joseph's gift of interpreting dreams, as seen in his interactions with Pharaoh's cupbearer and baker (Genesis 40:5-23), is a clear manifestation of divine providence. This ability is not just a skill but a spiritual gift from God, serving as a means through which God communicates His purposes and plans. Joseph's correct interpretation of these dreams is a testament to God's continued guidance and presence in his life.

The Role of Patience and Faith

Joseph's experience in prison is also a lesson in patience and enduring faith. Despite the accuracy of his interpretations and the promise of the cupbearer to remember him (Genesis 40:14), Joseph remains in prison for two more years (Genesis 41:1). This period of waiting, though difficult, exemplifies Joseph's patience and unwavering trust in God's timing.

Preparation for Greater Responsibilities

The time Joseph spends in prison serves as a period of preparation for his eventual elevation to a position of authority. The skills, wisdom, and spiritual insights he gains are crucial for the roles he is yet to assume. His experiences equip him with a unique perspective and understanding, preparing him for the complex tasks ahead, including the administration during the years of famine.

Divine Sovereignty and Human Responsibility

Joseph's story in prison highlights the interplay between divine sovereignty and human responsibility. While God's providential plan is overarching, Joseph's personal choices and actions play a crucial role in the unfolding of this plan. His consistent faithfulness and integrity, even in adverse circumstances, are instrumental in the realization of God's promises.

From Imprisonment to Exaltation

Joseph's eventual release and rise to power, beginning with his interpretation of Pharaoh's dreams (Genesis 41:14-

36), mark the transition from his trials to triumph. This shift is a powerful illustration of how God can elevate someone from the lowest of positions to the highest, in accordance with His sovereign plan.

The Interweaving of Providence and Purpose

Joseph's unjust imprisonment, viewed through the lens of divine providence, reveals the intricate ways in which God works through human circumstances to achieve His purposes. Joseph's journey from the pit to prison, and eventually to Pharaoh's court, is a testament to God's unfailing sovereignty, the importance of maintaining faith in the midst of trials, and the mysterious yet perfect alignment of God's timing and purposes in the lives of His faithful.

Joseph's Rise to Power in Egypt

The Divine Revelation Through Dreams

Joseph's ascent to power begins with Pharaoh's troubling dreams, which none of his wise men and magicians could interpret (Genesis 41:1-8). The biblical narrative illustrates the significance of dreams as a medium of divine revelation, a theme recurrent in Joseph's life. The inability of Egypt's wise men to interpret these dreams demonstrates the limitations of human wisdom and the supremacy of God's wisdom.

The Cupbearer's Recollection

Joseph's path to power is paved when the cupbearer, remembering Joseph's accurate interpretation of his own dream, recommends him to Pharaoh (Genesis 41:9-13). This moment is pivotal, as it signifies the fulfillment of God's promise and the unfolding of His plan for Joseph. It highlights the importance of God's timing in bringing to fruition His plans.

Interpreting Pharaoh's Dreams

Joseph's interpretation of Pharaoh's dreams (Genesis 41:14-32) showcases his spiritual discernment and reliance on God for wisdom. Joseph attributes the ability to interpret dreams to God (Genesis 41:16), underscoring his humility and recognition of God as the source of all wisdom. His interpretation reveals the forthcoming seven years of abundance followed by seven years of famine, demonstrating God's sovereignty over natural events and His foreknowledge.

The Proposal for Egypt's Salvation

Joseph's wisdom is further evident in his proposal to Pharaoh on how to deal with the impending famine (Genesis 41:33-36). His insight into resource management and planning showcases not only his administrative skills but also his concern for the well-being of Egypt and its people. This proposal reflects Joseph's understanding of stewardship and his ability to apply divine wisdom to practical governance.

Elevation to Power

Joseph's elevation to a position of authority over Egypt (Genesis 41:37-45) is a profound example of God exalting those who remain faithful to Him. Pharaoh recognizes Joseph's wisdom and discernment as divine, leading to his appointment as the second-in-command in Egypt. This appointment is not just a personal triumph for Joseph but a fulfillment of God's plan for him to save many lives.

Joseph's Administration During the Years of Abundance

During the seven years of abundance, Joseph's administrative abilities shine as he oversees the collection and storage of grain (Genesis 41:46-49). His foresight and effective management ensure Egypt is well-prepared for the coming famine. This period also reflects Joseph's obedience to God's instructions, a key aspect of his character.

The Famine Years and Joseph's Leadership

As the years of famine begin, Joseph's role becomes even more crucial. His distribution of stored grain saves not only Egypt but also neighboring regions from starvation (Genesis 41:53-57). Joseph's leadership during the famine demonstrates his compassion, wisdom, and the far-reaching impact of his God-given abilities.

Joseph's Brothers Come to Egypt

The arrival of Joseph's brothers in Egypt to buy grain (Genesis 42) marks a significant moment in the narrative. It sets the stage for reconciliation and the fulfillment of Joseph's earlier dreams. This encounter also tests Joseph's character and his forgiveness towards his brothers, who had wronged him.

Joseph's Recognition and Reconciliation with His Brothers

The eventual recognition and reconciliation between Joseph and his brothers (Genesis 45) is a powerful moment of grace and forgiveness. Joseph reveals his identity to his brothers and reassures them of his forgiveness, attributing the events to God's plan for good (Genesis 45:5-8). This reconciliation is a testament to Joseph's faith, his understanding of God's sovereignty, and his ability to see God's hand in his life's events.

Joseph's Rise as Part of God's Salvific Plan

Joseph's rise from slavery to royalty in Egypt is a remarkable story of faith, perseverance, and divine providence. It illustrates how God can use even the most adverse circumstances for His purposes. Joseph's journey demonstrates the sovereignty of God in salvation history, His ability to work through human events to bring about redemption, and the power of forgiveness and reconciliation. Joseph's life, therefore, stands as a profound testament to God's faithfulness and the unfolding of His redemptive plan through the lives of individuals.

Reconciliation and Preservation: Joseph's Role in God's Plan

The Fulfillment of Dreams and the Path to Reconciliation

Joseph's journey, from being sold into slavery to rising to power in Egypt, culminates in a poignant moment of reconciliation with his brothers. This event is not merely a family reunion; it is a fulfillment of the dreams Joseph had years before, which depicted his brothers bowing down to him (Genesis 37:5-11). The realization of these dreams in Genesis 42-45 is a testament to the accuracy of divine revelation and the sovereignty of God in orchestrating events.

Joseph's Recognition of Divine Providence

One of the most profound aspects of Joseph's story is his recognition of God's hand in his life's events. In Genesis 45:5-8, Joseph reassures his brothers that it was God who sent him ahead of them to preserve life. His ability to see past the immediate pain and injustice of his experiences and recognize God's greater purpose demonstrates a deep faith and understanding of divine sovereignty.

The Preservation of the Israelite Family Line

Joseph's role in God's plan extends beyond personal reconciliation. By providing for his family during the famine, he preserves the lineage through which God had promised to bless all nations – the lineage of Abraham, Isaac, and Jacob. This act of preservation is crucial in the unfolding narrative of salvation history, as it ensures the continuation of the line that would eventually lead to the birth of Jesus Christ.

Joseph as a Type of Christ

Joseph's life serves as a typology of Christ. Just as Joseph was betrayed and sold, Christ was betrayed and handed over to death. And, like Joseph who rose to a position of authority to save his people, Christ rose from the dead and was exalted, bringing salvation to humanity. Joseph's forgiveness and provision for his brothers prefigure Christ's forgiveness and provision for humanity's sins.

The Role of Forgiveness in God's Plan

The theme of forgiveness is central in Joseph's story. His forgiveness of his brothers, despite their grave betrayal, mirrors the forgiveness that is at the heart of the Christian message. Joseph's actions demonstrate the power of forgiveness in breaking cycles of retribution and in restoring broken relationships, which is fundamental to the concept of salvation.

The Wisdom of God in Human Affairs

Joseph's story is a powerful illustration of the wisdom of God working through human affairs. Every event, from Joseph's enslavement to his elevation, and finally to the family's relocation to Egypt, is part of a divine orchestration. These events highlight that God's ways and thoughts are higher than human ways and thoughts (Isaiah 55:8-9).

The Preservation of Life and the Preparing of a Nation

Joseph's role in God's plan is not only about preserving his immediate family but also about preparing a nation. The settlement of Jacob's family in Egypt sets the stage for the growth of the Israelites into a numerous people, as promised to Abraham (Genesis 15:5). This growth, while leading to their eventual enslavement, is also a necessary step in God's plan for forming a people through whom He would reveal His law and ultimately bring forth the Messiah.

Providence in the Midst of Suffering

A crucial lesson from Joseph's story is the understanding of divine providence in the midst of suffering. Joseph's hardships were integral to God's plan for his elevation and for the preservation of the Israelite family. This perspective offers profound insight into the nature of suffering and God's ability to use it for good, a theme echoed in the New Testament (Romans 8:28).

Conclusion: Joseph's Role in the Unfolding Plan of Salvation

Joseph's rise to power in Egypt and his subsequent actions of forgiveness and preservation play a pivotal role in the unfolding plan of salvation. His story is a vivid illustration of God's providence, the fulfillment of divine promises, and the centrality of forgiveness in the salvific narrative. Joseph's life, therefore, serves as a powerful example of faith, forgiveness, and the overarching sovereignty of God in the tapestry of salvation history.

EXPLAINING THE DOCTRINE OF SALVATION

CHAPTER 3: Exodus: Deliverance from Egyptian Bondage

The Israelites' Plight in Egypt

The Setting of Israelite Bondage

The plight of the Israelites in Egypt, as narrated in the Book of Exodus, begins with a dramatic shift in their circumstances. Following the death of Joseph and his generation, a new king arises in Egypt who does not know Joseph (Exodus 1:8). This change in leadership marks the beginning of a period of oppression and hardship for the Israelites, setting the stage for their eventual deliverance.

Increasing Oppression by the Egyptian Pharaoh

The Egyptian Pharaoh, feeling threatened by the growing number of Israelites, decides to oppress them and reduce their population (Exodus 1:9-10). This oppression includes forced labor, as the Israelites are put to work on Pharaoh's building projects and in his fields. The harshness of their labor is a deliberate attempt to crush their spirits and weaken them as a people (Exodus 1:11-14).

The Decree to Kill Hebrew Males

In a further act of oppression, Pharaoh commands the killing of all newborn Hebrew males (Exodus 1:15-16). This decree is a direct attack on the future of the Israelite people, aiming to diminish their numbers and prevent the rise of potential leaders who might oppose Egyptian rule. The midwives' refusal to carry out this order, fearing God more than Pharaoh (Exodus 1:17), highlights the moral dilemma and the bravery of those who stand against such tyranny.

The Condition of Slavery and its Impact

The condition of slavery imposed on the Israelites is characterized by brutality and humiliation. Their treatment at the hands of the Egyptian taskmasters is a testament to the cruelty of Pharaoh's regime. This period of suffering and bondage profoundly impacts the Israelite identity, fostering a sense of longing for deliverance and a return to the land promised to their forefathers.

The Cry for Deliverance

The Israelites' cry for deliverance is a significant theme in Exodus (Exodus 2:23-25). Their groaning under the weight of slavery and their cry for help reach God, who remembers His covenant with Abraham, Isaac, and Jacob. This divine remembrance is crucial, as it sets in motion the events leading to their liberation.

Moses – The Emergence of a Deliverer

The birth and early life of Moses are intricately linked to the Israelites' plight. His miraculous preservation after being placed in the Nile (Exodus 2:1-10) and his later experiences in Midian (Exodus 2:11-22) are preparatory steps for his role as the deliverer. Moses' encounter with God at the burning bush (Exodus 3) marks his commissioning as the leader who would confront Pharaoh and lead the Israelites out of bondage.

Theological Significance of the Israelites' Bondage

The Israelites' bondage in Egypt holds significant theological implications:

- It exemplifies the theme of suffering and the longing for redemption, a motif that recurs throughout the Bible.

- The bondage serves as a backdrop against which God's power and faithfulness are dramatically displayed in the Exodus.

- It foreshadows the spiritual bondage of sin from which Christ would deliver humanity.

The Role of Faith and Hope in Bondage

Despite their suffering, the Israelites maintain a sense of hope and faith in God's promises. This faith is not passive but is characterized by a fervent cry for deliverance and a clinging to the promises made to their ancestors. Their faith amidst suffering foreshadows the faith required for salvation in the Christian doctrine.

God's Response to the Israelites' Plight

God's response to the plight of the Israelites is a key aspect of the Exodus narrative. His intervention, characterized by mighty acts and judgments against Egypt, is a powerful testament to His commitment to His covenant and His compassion for His people.

The Plight as a Prelude to Deliverance

The Israelites' plight in Egypt is a prelude to one of the most significant acts of deliverance in the Old Testament. This period of oppression and suffering sets the stage for God's mighty acts of salvation, showcasing His power, justice, and faithfulness. The narrative serves as a foundational story of deliverance and redemption, echoing the greater salvation that would come through Jesus Christ, offering freedom from the bondage of sin.

The Call of Moses and Aaron

Moses: Early Life and Divine Preparation

Moses, born to a Hebrew family and raised in Pharaoh's palace, embodies a unique blend of Hebrew heritage and Egyptian upbringing (Exodus 2:1-10). This dual identity plays a crucial role in his preparation as the deliverer of Israel. Moses' early life, marked by an incident where he defends a Hebrew slave, leading to his flight to Midian (Exodus 2:11-15), signifies his inherent sense of justice and connection to his people.

The Burning Bush: A Pivotal Divine Encounter

Moses' encounter with God at the burning bush (Exodus 3:1-10) is a pivotal moment in the narrative of Exodus. Here, God reveals Himself to Moses, commissioning him to lead the Israelites out of Egypt. This encounter is significant for several reasons:

- It marks the first direct communication between God and Moses.

- God reveals His name, "I AM WHO I AM" (Yahweh), establishing a personal relationship with Moses.

- The burning bush, a symbol of God's holy presence, signifies His power and the miraculous nature of the mission.

Moses' Reluctance and God's Assurance

Moses initially expresses reluctance and inadequacy to carry out the mission (Exodus 3:11, 4:1, 4:10). His hesitancy reflects a common human response to divine calling. However, God reassures Moses, promising His presence and equipping him with signs and wonders to validate his mission (Exodus 3:12, 4:2-9).

The Role of Aaron

Aaron, Moses' brother, is brought into the narrative as Moses' spokesperson (Exodus 4:14-16). His inclusion addresses Moses' concern about his eloquence. Aaron's role is crucial in the initial confrontations with Pharaoh, as he serves as the mouthpiece for Moses, delivering God's message.

The Commission to Deliver Israel

Moses and Aaron's commission to deliver Israel from bondage is not merely a call to free them from physical slavery; it is a mandate to restore them to a covenant relationship with God. The deliverance from Egypt is intrinsically linked to the Israelites' identity as God's chosen people and their destiny in the Promised Land.

Confrontation with Pharaoh

The confrontations between Moses (and Aaron) and Pharaoh (Exodus 5-11) are marked by a series of demands to let the Israelites go, met with Pharaoh's stubborn refusal. Each refusal leads to a plague, demonstrating God's power over Egypt's gods and Pharaoh's impotence. These events highlight the themes of divine judgment, the sovereignty of God, and the liberation of His people.

Moses as a Leader and Mediator

Throughout the narrative, Moses emerges as a leader and mediator. His intercessory role is evident in his prayers for the cessation of the plagues (Exodus 8:12, 9:33) and his advocacy for the people in their disobedience (Exodus 32:11-14). Moses' leadership is characterized by humility, faith, and a deep sense of responsibility towards both God and his people.

Theological Significance of Moses and Aaron's Call

The call of Moses and Aaron carries significant theological implications:

- It demonstrates God's initiative in salvation history. God actively chooses and equips leaders to accomplish His redemptive purposes.

- It underscores the principle of divine selection. God often chooses unlikely candidates to fulfill His plans.

- It highlights the partnership between divine sovereignty and human agency. God's plans are executed through human instruments who respond in obedience.

Moses and Aaron as Forerunners of Christ

Moses and Aaron, in their roles as deliverer and high priest, respectively, prefigure aspects of Christ's ministry.

Moses as the deliverer and lawgiver foreshadows Christ's role as the ultimate Deliverer and the mediator of a new covenant (Hebrews 3:1-6). Aaron as the high priest symbolizes Christ's priestly role, making atonement for the sins of the people (Hebrews 4:14-16).

The Call as a Catalyst for Deliverance

The call of Moses and Aaron is a catalyst for the deliverance of the Israelites from Egyptian bondage. It marks the beginning of a significant phase in the history of Israel and in the unfolding narrative of salvation. Their story is a testament to God's power to save and His willingness to use flawed but willing individuals to achieve His redemptive purposes.

Confrontation with Pharaoh: The Ten Plagues

Introduction to the Ten Plagues

The confrontation between Moses (and Aaron) and Pharaoh, which leads to the Ten Plagues, is a critical juncture in the narrative of the Exodus. These plagues, sent by God, serve multiple purposes: they demonstrate His power, judge Egypt's false gods, and ultimately lead to the liberation of the Israelites. Each plague escalates in intensity and impact, underscoring the severity of Pharaoh's resistance and the might of God's intervention.

1. The Plague of Blood (Exodus 7:14-24)

The first plague turns the Nile River into blood, a direct assault on Egypt's life source and the deity Hapi, the god of the Nile. This plague disrupts the essential water supply, causing ecological and societal chaos. It sets the tone for the subsequent plagues and shows Pharaoh the power of the God of Israel.

2. The Plague of Frogs (Exodus 8:1-15)

The second plague brings an overwhelming infestation of frogs, associated with the goddess Heqet. Frogs invade every aspect of Egyptian life, causing distress and discomfort. Pharaoh's magicians replicate this plague, ironically adding to Egypt's misery, but it is Moses and Aaron who can make the frogs go away, demonstrating God's exclusive power to remove the plague.

3. The Plague of Gnats (Exodus 8:16-19)

The third plague, gnats from the dust of the ground, signifies a shift where Pharaoh's magicians can no longer replicate the plagues, acknowledging, "This is the finger of God." The inability of Egyptian sorcery to contend with this plague highlights the supremacy of the God of Israel.

4. The Plague of Flies (Exodus 8:20-32)

The fourth plague introduces a distinction between the Israelites and Egyptians, as God spares Goshen, where the Israelites live. This distinction emphasizes God's protection over His people amidst judgment.

5. The Plague on Livestock (Exodus 9:1-7)

The fifth plague causes the death of Egyptian livestock, a direct blow to Egypt's economy and to deities associated with animals, like Hathor. The distinction between Israelite and Egyptian livestock underlines God's precision in judgment.

6. The Plague of Boils (Exodus 9:8-12)

Boils afflict the Egyptians as the sixth plague, impacting health and reinforcing the impotence of Egyptian gods and magicians. This plague challenges the deity Sekhmet, associated with healing, and further hardens Pharaoh's heart.

7. The Plague of Hail (Exodus 9:13-35)

This severe weather phenomenon devastates Egypt's agriculture, targeting Nut, the sky goddess, and Osiris, linked to crop fertility. The warning given before this plague shows God's mercy, offering a chance for Egyptians to escape harm.

8. The Plague of Locusts (Exodus 10:1-20)

This plague consumes what was left from the hail, decimating Egypt's food supply. It symbolizes total ruin and further demonstrates the impotence of Egyptian deities against the God of Israel.

9. The Plague of Darkness (Exodus 10:21-29)

Darkness for three days is particularly significant as it defies Ra, the sun god, one of Egypt's primary deities. This supernatural darkness symbolizes the spiritual blindness and judgment upon Egypt.

10. The Plague of the Firstborn (Exodus 11:1-10, 12:29-32)

The final and most devastating plague results in the death of every firstborn in Egypt. It is a direct judgment against Pharaoh and all of Egypt for their oppression of God's people. This plague finally compels Pharaoh to release the Israelites.

Theological Significance of the Plagues

The plagues reveal several theological truths:

- God's sovereignty over nature and the impotence of false gods.

- The judgment of God upon sin and oppression.

- The redemption and separation of God's people from the world.

- The escalation of the plagues demonstrates God's increasing judgment in response to hardened hearts.

Moses and Aaron as Instruments of God's Will

Throughout the plagues, Moses and Aaron serve faithfully as instruments of God's will. Their obedience and courage in confronting Pharaoh are crucial in the fulfillment of God's plan for Israel's deliverance.

The Plagues as Prelude to Deliverance

The plagues set the stage for the ultimate deliverance of the Israelites. They demonstrate God's commitment to freeing His people and establishing them as a nation under His rule. The plagues, therefore, are not just punitive but are integral to the salvific journey of the Israelites, leading to the establishment of the Passover and the Exodus, pivotal events in Jewish and Christian theology.

The Ten Plagues in Salvation History

The Ten Plagues, as part of the Exodus narrative, hold a significant place in the history of salvation. They represent God's powerful intervention in human history to save His people, showcasing His might, judgment, and redemptive power. The story of the plagues, culminating in the Exodus, serves as a testament to God's faithfulness to His promises and His sovereign ability to deliver and redeem.

The Miraculous Crossing of the Red Sea

The Context of the Red Sea Crossing

The crossing of the Red Sea is one of the most pivotal events in the Exodus narrative, symbolizing God's power to deliver and protect His people. Following the Ten Plagues and Pharaoh's reluctant release of the Israelites, they find themselves trapped between the advancing Egyptian army and the Red Sea (Exodus 14:1-9). This moment sets the stage for a profound demonstration of God's salvation.

God's Strategy and the Pillar of Cloud and Fire

As the Israelites camp by the sea, God leads them by a pillar of cloud by day and a pillar of fire by night, symbolizing His presence and guidance (Exodus 13:21-22). This divine guidance is not only a physical leading but also a spiritual reassurance of God's protection and sovereignty.

Pharaoh's Pursuit and Israel's Desperation

Pharaoh's decision to pursue the Israelites (Exodus 14:5-9) reveals the hardening of his heart and his inability to recognize God's supremacy. The Israelites, seeing the approaching Egyptian forces, react with fear and despair, questioning Moses' leadership and God's plan (Exodus 14:10-12). This fear and doubt exemplify the human tendency to despair in the face of seemingly insurmountable challenges.

Moses' Faith and Divine Assurance

In response to the Israelites' fear, Moses encourages them to stand firm and trust in God's deliverance (Exodus 14:13-14). His statement, "The Lord will fight for you, and you have only to be silent," reflects profound faith in God's power and faithfulness. This trust is a key element in understanding the nature of divine salvation.

The Miraculous Parting of the Red Sea

The parting of the Red Sea, as Moses stretches out his hand over the sea at God's command (Exodus 14:15-21), is a powerful miracle demonstrating God's control over nature. The creation of a dry path through the sea illustrates that God's methods of deliverance often surpass human understanding.

The Israelites' Passage and Egyptian Destruction

The Israelites' safe passage through the Red Sea on dry ground (Exodus 14:22) symbolizes deliverance from bondage and the transition to freedom. The subsequent destruction of the Egyptian army, as the waters return to their place (Exodus 14:26-28), signifies the final act of liberation from Egyptian oppression and a judgment against those who opposed God's will.

Theological Significance of the Red Sea Crossing

The crossing of the Red Sea holds deep theological significance:

- It represents God's power to save and His ability to make a way where there seems to be no way.

- The event serves as a metaphor for baptism, symbolizing the believers' passage from death to life in Christ (1 Corinthians 10:1-2).

- It demonstrates God's faithfulness and His commitment to fulfilling His promises.

A Manifestation of God's Glory

The Red Sea crossing reveals God's glory and serves as a testimony to His name among the nations (Exodus 14:4, 18). It is a demonstration of His supremacy over earthly powers and false gods, affirming His identity as the one true God.

The Response of the Israelites: Faith and Worship

The safe crossing and the destruction of the Egyptians lead to a response of faith and worship among the Israelites. The Song of Moses (Exodus 15:1-21) reflects their awe and gratitude for God's deliverance, affirming their trust in Him as their strength and salvation.

The Red Sea Crossing in Salvation History

The crossing of the Red Sea is a cornerstone event in salvation history, encapsulating themes of deliverance, faith, judgment, and the fulfillment of God's promises. It prefigures the greater salvation in Christ, offering spiritual liberation from sin and death. The narrative of the Red Sea crossing stands as an enduring testament to God's power, faithfulness, and His unwavering commitment to the salvation of His people.

The Journey to the Promised Land: Guidance and Provision

The Exodus: Beginning of the Journey

The Exodus from Egypt marks the beginning of a significant journey for the Israelites, not just in a geographical sense but also in their spiritual and covenantal relationship with God. This journey, which ultimately leads to the Promised Land, is characterized by God's continuous guidance and provision, testing and shaping the nation of Israel into a people of faith.

Guidance by God: Pillar of Cloud and Fire

One of the most striking aspects of this journey is the divine guidance provided by God. The Israelites are led by a pillar of cloud by day and a pillar of fire by night (Exodus 13:21-22). This miraculous guidance serves multiple purposes: it assures the Israelites of God's presence, provides them with direction, and offers protection against potential enemies and natural elements.

Crossing the Red Sea: A Defining Moment

The crossing of the Red Sea (Exodus 14) is a defining moment in the journey. It represents not only a physical deliverance from Egyptian pursuit but also a spiritual passage from slavery to freedom. This miraculous event symbolizes baptism into Moses (1 Corinthians 10:2), an allegory for the Christian baptism and passage from sin to salvation through Christ.

Manna and Quail: Provision in the Wilderness

The provision of manna and quail (Exodus 16) is a testament to God's care and provision. Despite the Israelites' complaints and doubts, God faithfully provides for their needs. The manna, appearing six days a week with a double portion before the Sabbath, also teaches the Israelites to rely on God's daily provision and observe the Sabbath, reinforcing key aspects of their covenant relationship with Him.

Water from the Rock: Meeting Physical and Spiritual Needs

The miraculous provision of water from the rock at Horeb (Exodus 17:1-7) not only meets a physical need but also symbolizes the spiritual sustenance that God provides. This event prefigures Christ as the spiritual rock that accompanies believers, providing living water (1 Corinthians 10:4; John 4:10-14).

The Giving of the Law at Sinai

The giving of the Law at Mount Sinai (Exodus 19-20) is a pivotal event in the journey. The Law, including the Ten Commandments, establishes the foundation of the covenant between God and Israel. It defines the moral, social, and ceremonial aspects of Israel's relationship with God and sets the standard for their conduct as a holy nation.

The Tabernacle: God's Dwelling Among His People

The construction of the Tabernacle (Exodus 25-31, 35-40) signifies God's desire to dwell among His people. The Tabernacle serves as a visible reminder of God's presence and as a central place of worship and sacrifice. It foreshadows the temple and ultimately, the incarnation of Christ, God dwelling among humanity (John 1:14).

Testing and Rebellion

The journey to the Promised Land is also marked by moments of testing and rebellion, such as the incident with the golden calf (Exodus 32) and the complaints and disobedience of the people (e.g., Numbers 14). These events reveal the Israelites' struggle to trust and obey God, reflecting humanity's broader struggle with faith and obedience.

Leadership of Moses and Aaron

Throughout the journey, the leadership of Moses and Aaron is instrumental. Moses, in particular, stands as a mediator between God and the people, interceding on their behalf and guiding them according to God's command. Their leadership, despite challenges, is crucial in steering the nation towards their covenantal destiny.

Preparation for Entering the Promised Land

The journey, with its trials and triumphs, prepares the Israelites for entering the Promised Land. It is a process of transformation, where a group of slaves becomes a covenant nation, ready to inherit the land promised to their forefathers. This transformation is both a physical journey and a spiritual pilgrimage, shaping their identity and faith.

Conclusion: The Journey as a Metaphor for Salvation

The journey of the Israelites to the Promised Land is a powerful metaphor for the Christian journey of salvation. It encapsulates themes of redemption, divine guidance and provision, covenant relationship, testing and obedience, and the ultimate goal of entering the promised rest. This narrative serves as a profound illustration of God's plan of salvation, His faithfulness to His promises, and the journey of faith each believer undertakes in Christ.

Edward D. Andrews

CHAPTER 4: Salvation in the Time of Judges: The Story of Gideon

Israel's Cycle of Apostasy and Oppression

Introduction to the Era of the Judges

The period of the Judges, as depicted in the book of Judges, is characterized by a cyclical pattern of Israelite behavior: apostasy, oppression, repentance, and deliverance. This cycle is a recurring theme throughout the book, highlighting the Israelites' fluctuating faithfulness to God and His continual mercy in raising up deliverers, or judges, to rescue them.

The Nature of Israelite Apostasy

Apostasy in the time of the Judges refers to the Israelites' abandonment of their covenant with God. This abandonment often involved the worship of Canaanite deities like Baal and Asherah (Judges 2:11-13). Such idolatry was a direct violation of the first commandment and represented a fundamental breach in their relationship with God.

The Consequences of Apostasy: Divine Judgment

The Israelites' idolatry and abandonment of God's laws inevitably led to divine judgment. This judgment typically came in the form of oppression by surrounding nations. The book of Judges describes a series of foreign oppressions as a direct consequence of Israel's sin, illustrating the principle that sin leads to bondage and suffering.

Oppression as a Means of Divine Discipline

The oppression of Israel by neighboring nations served as a form of divine discipline. It was intended to bring the Israelites to a realization of their sins and their need for repentance. This divine discipline was not merely punitive but was aimed at restoring the covenant relationship between God and His people.

The Role of the Judges

In response to the Israelites' cries for help, God raised up judges to deliver them from their oppressors. These judges were not just military leaders but also served as spiritual leaders who called the people back to faithfulness to God. The story of Gideon, in particular, illustrates this dual role.

Gideon's Call and Reluctance

Gideon's story begins with his call by God to deliver Israel from Midianite oppression (Judges 6:11-16). Gideon's initial reluctance and request for signs reflect the Israelites' weakened faith and the need for reassurance of God's presence and power.

The Significance of Gideon's Fleece

Gideon's request for a sign using a fleece (Judges 6:36-40) is often interpreted as a lack of faith. However, it can also be seen as a desire for confirmation of God's will in a time of uncertainty. This incident highlights the challenges of discerning God's will and the human need for assurance in carrying out God's commands.

Dismantling Idolatry: The Altar of Baal

Before leading Israel into battle, Gideon is commanded to tear down his father's altar to Baal and build an altar to the Lord (Judges 6:25-32). This act symbolizes the need to remove idolatry and re-establish worship of the true God as a precursor to deliverance.

The Victory over the Midianites

The victory of Gideon and his 300 men over the Midianites (Judges 7) is a remarkable demonstration of God's power. The drastic reduction of Gideon's army and the unconventional tactics used highlight that the victory is attributed to God, not human strength or wisdom.

The Cycle of Apostasy Post-Gideon

After Gideon's death, Israel falls back into the cycle of apostasy (Judges 8:33-34). This recurrent theme in Judges emphasizes the constant struggle to maintain faithfulness to God and the ease with which people can revert to idolatry.

Theological Implications

The cycle of apostasy and oppression in the time of the Judges has profound theological implications:

- It demonstrates the inherent human tendency to stray from God and the consequences of such disobedience.

- It highlights God's mercy and patience in repeatedly delivering His people despite their unfaithfulness.

- It underscores the necessity of divine intervention for true deliverance, a theme that culminates in the New Testament with the ultimate deliverance through Jesus Christ.

Lessons from the Time of Judges

The era of the Judges, particularly the story of Gideon, teaches critical lessons about the nature of faith, the consequences of apostasy, and the continual need for divine deliverance. It serves as a reminder of the human propensity towards sin, the necessity of repentance, and the graciousness of God in providing salvation, pointing ultimately to the need for a permanent solution to sin, which is found in Jesus Christ.

Gideon's Call and Divine Assurance

The Context of Gideon's Call

Gideon's story unfolds during a time of great distress for Israel, under the oppressive rule of the Midianites. This period is marked by Israel's repeated cycle of sin, suffering, repentance, and deliverance. Gideon's call is set against this backdrop of Israelite apostasy and its consequences.

Gideon's Initial Encounter with the Angel of the Lord

Gideon's divine calling occurs while he is threshing wheat in a winepress, an act that reflects the fear and oppression the Israelites are experiencing (Judges 6:11). The appearance of the Angel of the Lord to Gideon is both unexpected and momentous. The Angel greets him as a "mighty warrior" and assures him of the Lord's presence (Judges 6:12), a greeting that stands in contrast to Gideon's current situation and self-perception.

Gideon's Questioning and God's Response

Gideon questions why the Israelites are suffering if the Lord is with them (Judges 6:13). His questioning reveals a struggle to reconcile the reality of their suffering with the covenant promises of God. In response, God does not rebuke Gideon but instead calls him to action, stating, "Go in the strength you have and save Israel out of Midian's hand" (Judges 6:14). This response indicates that God's deliverance often comes through human agents empowered by Him.

The Assurance of God's Presence

Gideon is assured of God's presence with the words, "I will be with you" (Judges 6:16). This promise is the cornerstone of Gideon's call and is crucial for understanding his subsequent actions. It emphasizes that divine calling goes hand in hand with divine empowerment.

Gideon's Request for a Sign

Gideon's request for a sign to confirm his calling (Judges 6:17) reflects a common biblical theme where individuals seek confirmation of God's will. This request is not necessarily indicative of a lack of faith but rather a desire for assurance in carrying out a daunting task. The sign given – fire consuming the offering – reaffirms God's presence and calling (Judges 6:21).

Dismantling the Altar of Baal

Before leading Israel into battle, Gideon is commanded to tear down his father's altar to Baal and build a proper altar to God (Judges 6:25-27). This act symbolizes the rejection of idolatry and a return to true worship, serving as a foundational step for the Israelites' deliverance.

The Fleece Test: Seeking Further Confirmation

Gideon's fleece test (Judges 6:36-40) is often interpreted as a manifestation of his doubt. However, it can also be seen as an example of Gideon seeking further assurance for a daunting task. The specific nature of the fleece test – seeking a sign involving dew and dryness – reveals Gideon's desire for clear, unmistakable guidance from God. The test is not so much a challenge to God's power but a request for confirmation in a situation where much is at stake. The fact that God responds to Gideon's request not once but twice, first with dew on the fleece only and then with dew on the ground only, demonstrates God's patience and willingness to reassure His chosen servant.

Theological Implications of the Fleece Test

The fleece test has significant theological implications. It illustrates the personal nature of God's relationship with His people, where He addresses individual fears and needs. This incident also shows that God's calling often comes with challenges that require faith and reliance on divine assurance. Moreover, it underscores the principle that God's purposes can be fulfilled through imperfect faith, as He works through human frailty and doubts.

Gideon's Transformation and Leadership

The transformation in Gideon, from a hesitant individual to a confident leader, is remarkable. Post the fleece test, Gideon exhibits decisive leadership, rallying the Israelites against Midian (Judges 7:1-25). His strategy and reliance on God rather than conventional military might – reducing his army to just 300 men – underscore his complete trust in God's guidance and power.

Divine Strategy in Battle

The battle against the Midianites, where Gideon and his small army emerge victorious, is a powerful testament to the effectiveness of divine strategy over human strength. The unconventional tactics, involving trumpets, jars, and torches, lead to confusion and defeat among the Midianites. This victory is a clear demonstration of God's deliverance through means beyond human understanding.

Gideon as a Model of Faithful Service

Gideon's story is an exemplary model of faithful service to God. Despite initial doubts and fears, his willingness to obey and trust in God's promises makes him a significant figure in the narrative of Israel's salvation. His life illustrates the journey of faith – from questioning and uncertainty to trust and obedience.

Gideon's Legacy in Israel's Salvation History

Gideon's legacy in the context of Israel's salvation history is multifaceted. He emerges as a deliverer at a time when Israel is mired in idolatry and oppression. His leadership not only brings military victory but also spiritual renewal, at least for a time. Gideon's story contributes to the overarching biblical theme of God using flawed but willing individuals to achieve His redemptive purposes.

Divine Assurance in the Midst of Uncertainty

Gideon's call and the divine assurance he receives highlight a fundamental truth in the narrative of salvation: God often chooses unlikely candidates to fulfill His purposes and equips them for their mission. Gideon's story underscores the importance of seeking and trusting in God's guidance, especially when facing overwhelming challenges. His journey from doubt to faith mirrors the spiritual journey of believers, emphasizing reliance on God's power and presence for the accomplishment of His divine will.

The Reduction of Gideon's Army

The narrative of Gideon's army begins after Gideon receives assurance of victory from God. He gathers a large army to confront the Midianites, who have oppressed Israel.

Initially, Gideon's army numbers 32,000 men, a seemingly substantial force for the impending battle (Judges 7:3).

Divine Command to Reduce the Numbers

God, however, instructs Gideon to reduce his army. The Lord's rationale for this reduction is clear: "The people with you are too many for me to give the Midianites into their hand, lest Israel boast over me, saying, 'My own hand has saved me'" (Judges 7:2). This command underscores a recurring theme in the Bible: God's desire to ensure that His actions are recognized as the source of deliverance, not human might or numbers.

First Reduction: The Test of Fear

The first reduction of the army comes through a test of fear. Gideon is told to proclaim that anyone who is fearful and trembling may return home. As a result, 22,000 men depart, leaving only 10,000 (Judges 7:3). This reduction not only fulfills God's command but also ensures that the remaining soldiers are those with a greater degree of courage and trust in God.

Second Reduction: The Water Test

The second and more remarkable reduction occurs at the water. God instructs Gideon to observe how the men drink from the water and separates them based on this behavior. Those who lap the water with their hands to their mouths are set apart from those who kneel down to drink directly from the stream. Only 300 men pass this test, forming the final size of Gideon's army (Judges 7:5-7).

Symbolism of the Water Test

The water test is significant for several reasons:

- It may have been a test of vigilance and readiness for battle. Those who lapped the water like a dog were likely more alert and prepared for sudden attack.

- The method of drinking water was a seemingly arbitrary criterion, emphasizing that God's choices often transcend human understanding.

- The test illustrates the principle of divine selection, where God chooses based on His criteria, which may not align with human expectations or standards.

Gideon's Faith and Obedience

Gideon's compliance with God's command to reduce his army is a testament to his faith and obedience. Despite the apparent military disadvantage, Gideon trusts in God's promise of victory. His obedience is an act of faith in God's power and wisdom.

God's Power in Human Weakness

The reduction of Gideon's army to 300 men highlights a key biblical theme: God's power made perfect in human weakness (2 Corinthians 12:9). By reducing the army to a size that made victory seem humanly impossible, God ensures that the victory can only be attributed to divine intervention.

Preparation for the Battle

With the reduced army, Gideon prepares for battle. God provides Gideon with a strategy that relies not on conventional warfare but on unconventional tactics involving trumpets, jars, and torches (Judges 7:16-22). This approach further underscores the reliance on divine guidance rather than military might.

The Victory over the Midianites

The victory of Gideon's 300 men over the Midianite army is a dramatic demonstration of God's power. The Midianites are thrown into confusion and turn on each other, leading to their defeat (Judges 7:22). This outcome solidifies the understanding that the battle was won not by human strength but by the hand of God.

Theological Implications of the Army's Reduction

The reduction of Gideon's army and the subsequent victory carry profound theological implications:

- They reaffirm the sovereignty of God in salvation and deliverance.

- They exemplify the principle that God's ways are not human ways, and His thoughts are not human thoughts (Isaiah 55:8-9).

- They serve as a reminder of the importance of faith and reliance on God rather than on human resources or strategies.

Edward D. Andrews

Gideon's Army as a Model of Divine Deliverance

The story of the reduction of Gideon's army is a powerful illustration of divine deliverance and the principle that God often uses the weak and the few to accomplish His purposes. It challenges the conventional reliance on numbers and strength, pointing instead to the necessity of faith, obedience, and reliance on God's power. The narrative serves as a poignant reminder of the supremacy of God in the affairs of men and His ability to achieve victory in seemingly impossible circumstances.

The Victory over the Midianites

Setting the Stage for Battle

The story of Gideon's victory over the Midianites, as detailed in Judges 7, is a remarkable demonstration of God's power and providence. This victory is significant not only for its immediate impact on the Israelites but also for its theological implications in the broader narrative of salvation history.

The Disadvantageous Position

Gideon and his reduced army of 300 men find themselves in a seemingly disadvantageous position against the Midianites. The Midianites, along with their allies the Amalekites and others, are described as numerous as locusts, with camels as countless as the sand on the seashore (Judges 7:12). This description sets the scene for a battle that, in human terms, appears unwinnable for Gideon and his small force.

The Night Before the Battle

The night before the battle, God instructs Gideon to go down to the Midianite camp, where he overhears a conversation that reaffirms God's promise of victory (Judges 7:9-15). This incident serves to strengthen Gideon's faith and resolve, demonstrating how God provides assurance in times of uncertainty.

God's Unconventional Battle Plan

The strategy for the battle, as divinely instructed, is unconventional. Gideon's men are equipped not with traditional weapons but with trumpets, jars, and torches (Judges 7:16-18). This approach is a radical departure from conventional warfare tactics and underscores the principle that the battle is the Lord's, not dependent on human strength or weapons.

The Attack and the Midianites' Confusion

At Gideon's signal, his men break the jars, blow the trumpets, and shout, "A sword for the Lord and for Gideon!" (Judges 7:20). The sudden noise and the unexpected sight cause panic and confusion among the Midianites, leading them to turn on each other. This confusion is a direct result of divine intervention, causing the enemy forces to self-destruct.

Edward D. Andrews

The Role of Faith and Obedience

Gideon's faith and obedience are key to this victory. His willingness to follow God's instructions, despite their unconventional nature, is a testament to his trust in God. Gideon's leadership, based on faith rather than military acumen, becomes a model for understanding God's ways in achieving victory.

Theological Significance of the Victory

The victory over the Midianites holds several theological significances:

- It demonstrates God's power to save and deliver through means beyond human understanding.

- The victory serves as a testament to God's faithfulness to His promises and His care for His people.

- It illustrates the biblical theme of God achieving great victories through small or weak instruments, emphasizing His sovereignty and the principle of His strength in human weakness.

Echoes of the Victory in Salvation History

The victory over the Midianites echoes throughout salvation history. It prefigures the ultimate victory of God over sin and death achieved through Jesus Christ. Just as Gideon's victory was won not by human strength but by divine intervention, so is the victory over sin and death won by Christ's sacrificial death and resurrection, not by human efforts.

The Impact on the Israelites

The victory has a profound impact on the Israelites. It liberates them from Midianite oppression and leads to a period of peace. This deliverance reestablishes Israel's covenant relationship with God, reminding them of His lordship and their identity as His chosen people.

Gideon's Legacy

Gideon's legacy extends beyond his lifetime. He is remembered as a judge who, despite initial hesitance, rose to the challenge and delivered Israel through faith and reliance on God. His story serves as an enduring lesson on the importance of trusting in God's power and guidance.

The Victory Over the Midianites as a Paradigm of Divine Salvation

The story of Gideon's victory over the Midianites stands as a paradigm of divine salvation. It exemplifies how God works through unlikely means and people to achieve His purposes. This narrative reinforces the recurring biblical theme that God's ways often defy human logic, and His plans are accomplished not by might or power but by His Spirit. The victory, thus, serves as a powerful reminder of God's sovereignty in the affairs of nations and individuals, and His ability to bring deliverance in the most daunting circumstances.

Gideon's Legacy and Israel's Temporary Peace

The Aftermath of Victory

Following Gideon's victory over the Midianites, Israel experiences a period of peace that lasts for 40 years (Judges 8:28). This period of tranquility is significant in the turbulent era of the Judges, marking a temporary cessation of the cycle of apostasy and oppression that characterizes the period.

Gideon's Leadership and Governance

After the battle, the Israelites ask Gideon to rule over them, along with his sons, in a hereditary monarchy (Judges 8:22). Gideon, however, refuses, insisting that the Lord should rule over Israel. This refusal demonstrates Gideon's understanding of Israel's unique identity as a theocracy. Despite his refusal of kingship, Gideon exercises leadership in Israel during this period of peace, steering the nation back towards faithfulness to God.

The Ephod and Its Implications

Gideon makes an ephod out of the gold won in battle and places it in his hometown, Ophrah (Judges 8:27). While his intentions might have been to commemorate the victory or to facilitate worship, the ephod becomes a snare to Gideon and his family, leading to idolatry. This incident highlights the subtle ways in which even well-intentioned acts can lead to sin and underscores the persistent danger of idolatry for Israel.

Gideon's Personal Life and Its Impact

Gideon's personal life, particularly his many wives and concubines, and the large number of children he fathers (Judges 8:30-31), reflects the cultural practices of the time. However, it also sets the stage for future conflict, as seen in the story of his son Abimelech (Judges 9), who seeks to establish himself as king, leading to strife and bloodshed.

Gideon's Death and Israel's Relapse into Idolatry

Gideon's death marks the end of a period of relative faithfulness and peace in Israel. The Israelites quickly relapse into idolatry, worshipping the Baals and forgetting the Lord who had delivered them from their enemies (Judges 8:33-34). This rapid return to idolatry after Gideon's death illustrates the fragile nature of Israel's commitment to God, heavily dependent on the influence of their leaders.

Gideon's Legacy in Biblical Narrative

Gideon's legacy is complex. On one hand, he is remembered as a faithful judge who, despite initial hesitation, delivered Israel through God's power. His faith and obedience in the face of overwhelming odds are commendable. On the other hand, his actions in making the ephod and the consequences of his personal choices add a layer of ambiguity to his legacy.

Gideon as a Foreshadowing of Christ

In Christian theology, Gideon can be seen as a foreshadowing of Christ. Like Gideon, Jesus achieves victory not through conventional means but through the power of God. However, unlike Gideon, Christ establishes a lasting peace and deliverance, not just from physical oppression but from the bondage of sin and death.

Theological Reflections on Gideon's Story

Gideon's story raises several theological reflections:

- The necessity of God's power over human strength in achieving divine purposes.

- The constant need for vigilance against idolatry and sin.

- The importance of godly leadership in guiding and maintaining the faithfulness of God's people.

- The temporary nature of human deliverance compared to the eternal salvation offered in Christ.

The Enduring Lessons from Gideon's Life

Gideon's life and the period of peace that follows his victory offer enduring lessons for understanding God's salvation. His story is a testament to God's power working through flawed human beings and the ongoing struggle against sin and unfaithfulness. Gideon's narrative underscores the need for continual reliance on God and the importance of faithful leadership in maintaining a covenant relationship with Him. In the broader context of salvation history, Gideon's story points to the need for a perfect and lasting deliverer, fulfilled in Jesus Christ.

CHAPTER 5: The End of Exile: Liberation from Babylonian Captivity

The Babylonian Exile: Punishment and Prophecy

The Historical Context of the Babylonian Exile

The Babylonian Exile, a pivotal event in Jewish history, began in 586 BCE with the destruction of Jerusalem and the Temple by Nebuchadnezzar, king of Babylon. This catastrophic event was not merely a political disaster but had deep religious and theological implications for the people of Judah.

The Exile as Divine Punishment

The Exile is portrayed in the Hebrew Bible as divine punishment for the persistent idolatry and disobedience of the people of Judah (2 Chronicles 36:15-16). Prophets like Jeremiah and Ezekiel attribute the Exile to the people's failure to uphold the covenant with God, particularly their neglect of justice, mercy, and worship. This punishment is understood as a corrective measure, intended to bring the people back to a faithful relationship with God.

Prophetic Warnings Preceding the Exile

Prior to the Exile, prophets such as Isaiah, Jeremiah, and Ezekiel warned the people of impending judgment due to their sins. These prophecies highlight the inevitability of the Exile due to the people's refusal to repent. The prophets, however, also spoke of hope and restoration, assuring that the Exile would not be the end of God's people.

The Experience of Exile

The Exile was a period of profound crisis for the Israelites. It involved not only physical displacement but also a theological and existential crisis. The loss of the land, Temple, and Davidic monarchy challenged the foundational aspects of Israelite identity and faith. In Babylon, the Israelites had to renegotiate their understanding of God, community, and covenant in a foreign land.

Emergence of New Forms of Worship and Community

In the absence of the Temple and its rituals, the Exile led to the development of new forms of worship and community life. Synagogues and scripture study became central aspects of Jewish religious life, laying the foundation for Rabbinic Judaism. This period saw the compilation and preservation of many biblical texts, which played a crucial role in maintaining the faith and identity of the Jewish people.

The Role of Prophets During the Exile

Prophets like Ezekiel and Daniel played critical roles during the Exile. They provided guidance, hope, and a re-interpretation of Israel's relationship with God. Ezekiel's vision of the valley of dry bones (Ezekiel 37) symbolized the future restoration and revival of Israel. Daniel's faith and integrity in the Babylonian court exemplified steadfastness in the midst of a pagan society.

Prophecies of Restoration and Return

The Exile was also a time of prophetic promises of restoration and return. Jeremiah's prophecy of a new covenant (Jeremiah 31:31-34) and Isaiah's visions of a restored Jerusalem (Isaiah 40-55) offered hope for a future where the relationship between God and His people would be renewed.

The Role of Cyrus the Great

The end of the Babylonian Exile came with the rise of Cyrus the Great of Persia, who conquered Babylon in 539

BCE. Cyrus' decree allowing the Jews to return to Jerusalem and rebuild the Temple (Ezra 1:1-4) was seen as a fulfillment of God's promise to restore His people. Cyrus is portrayed as a messianic figure in Isaiah 45:1, being used by God to deliver His people.

Theological Significance of the Exile

The Babylonian Exile holds profound theological significance:

- It reaffirms the concept of covenantal relationship, where obedience to God leads to blessing, and disobedience leads to judgment.

- The Exile underscores the sovereignty of God over history and nations.

- It highlights the resilience and adaptability of faith in times of crisis.

- The Exile serves as a powerful illustration of God's discipline, but also His unfailing love and commitment to restoration.

The Exile as a Catalyst for Transformation

The Babylonian Exile was a catalyst for significant transformation in Jewish religious thought and practice. It was a period of both judgment and renewal, serving as a turning point that reshaped the trajectory of Jewish faith and identity. The Exile underscores the themes of punishment for sin, the faithfulness of God even in judgment, and the hope of restoration. These themes resonate throughout the biblical narrative of salvation, pointing to the ultimate restoration and redemption through Jesus Christ.

The Rise of the Medo-Persian Empire

A Shift in World Power

The rise of the Medo-Persian Empire marks a significant shift in the ancient Near East's political and cultural landscape. This transition played a crucial role in ending the Babylonian Exile of the Jewish people and set the stage for the return and restoration of Israel.

The Historical Background

The Medo-Persian Empire emerged as a dominant power in the 6th century BCE, overthrowing the Neo-Babylonian Empire. This change was initiated by Cyrus the Great, who founded the Achaemenid Empire, commonly known as the Persian Empire.

Cyrus the Great: A Key Figure

Cyrus the Great is a central figure in the narrative of the Jewish return from exile. Known for his policy of tolerance and diplomatic governance, Cyrus conquered Babylon in 539 BCE. His approach to empire-building marked a departure from the oppressive policies of the Babylonians, favoring instead a model of respect and autonomy for various peoples under his rule.

The Cyrus Cylinder and Biblical Prophecy

The Cyrus Cylinder, an ancient clay artifact, confirms the biblical account of Cyrus's decree to allow exiled peoples, including the Jews, to return to their homelands and rebuild their temples. This decree is remarkably consistent with the portrayal of Cyrus in the Bible, particularly in the book of Ezra (Ezra 1:1-4). Isaiah's prophecy, which names Cyrus as the Lord's anointed (Isaiah 45:1), predates his reign and highlights the sovereignty of God in using a Persian king to fulfill divine purposes.

Impact on the Jewish Exiles

Cyrus's decree had a profound impact on the Jewish community in Babylon. It not only allowed for their physical return to Judah but also signified a spiritual restoration. The return from exile was seen as a fulfillment of God's promises and a pivotal moment in salvation history, demonstrating God's faithfulness to His covenant people.

Rebuilding Jerusalem and the Temple

The return of the Jewish exiles under leaders like Zerubbabel, Ezra, and Nehemiah led to the rebuilding of Jerusalem and the Second Temple. This restoration was not just a physical reconstruction but also a spiritual renewal, as the people recommitted themselves to the Law of Moses.

The Medo-Persian Policy of Tolerance

The Medo-Persian Empire's policy of tolerance and respect for local customs and religions was instrumental in the survival and flourishing of Jewish culture and religious practices. This policy contrasts with the assimilationist and often oppressive approaches of other empires, providing a conducive environment for the Jewish people to retain their identity and traditions.

Theological Significance of the Medo-Persian Empire

Theologically, the rise of the Medo-Persian Empire and the subsequent end of the Babylonian Exile affirm several key themes:

God's sovereignty over nations and kings: The rise of Cyrus and his policies were seen as orchestrated by God for the fulfillment of His promises.

The fulfillment of prophecy: Cyrus's role in liberating the Jews aligns with prophetic writings, underscoring the accuracy and divine inspiration of biblical prophecy.

Restoration and redemption: The return from exile symbolizes God's redemptive plan for His people, foreshadowing the ultimate redemption through Jesus Christ.

The Medo-Persian Empire in Salvation History

The rise of the Medo-Persian Empire and its role in ending the Babylonian Exile is a significant chapter in the narrative of salvation history. It exemplifies God's providential guidance in historical events and His faithfulness to His people. The period of restoration that follows the exile sets the stage for the development of Second Temple Judaism and paves the way for the coming of Christ, the ultimate fulfillment of God's promise of salvation and restoration.

The Fall of Babylon: A Fulfillment of Prophecy

Introduction to Babylon's Fall

The fall of Babylon in 539 BCE marks a significant turning point in biblical history. This event is not only a major geopolitical shift but also a fulfillment of biblical prophecy, underscoring the theme of God's sovereignty over nations and the fulfillment of His divine purposes.

Babylon in Biblical Context

Babylon, a dominant empire in the ancient Near East, became a symbol of power, pride, and oppression in the biblical narrative. Its conquest of Jerusalem in 586 BCE and the subsequent exile of the Jewish people are pivotal events in the Old Testament.

Prophetic Foretellings of Babylon's Fall

Several prophets, notably Isaiah and Jeremiah, prophesied the downfall of Babylon. Isaiah spoke of Babylon's demise centuries before it occurred (Isaiah 13-14), depicting it as a judgment from God for its arrogance and idolatry. Jeremiah prophesied that Babylon, which was used as an instrument of God's judgment against Judah, would itself be judged and overthrown (Jeremiah 50-51).

The Historical Fall of Babylon

The historical fall of Babylon to Cyrus the Great of Persia was swift and relatively bloodless. According to historical records, the city fell without a major battle, as

Cyrus' army diverted the Euphrates River, allowing them to enter the city through the dried riverbed. This strategy was alluded to in Isaiah's prophecy, which mentions the drying up of Babylon's waters (Isaiah 44:27).

Theological Interpretation of the Fall

Theologically, Babylon's fall is interpreted as God's judgment on a nation that epitomized pride, idolatry, and oppression. It serves as a testament to the fact that no empire, no matter how powerful, is beyond the reach of God's judgment.

Cyrus as God's Instrument

Cyrus is portrayed in the Bible not merely as a conquering ruler but as an instrument of God's will. Isaiah refers to Cyrus as God's "anointed" (Isaiah 45:1), a term typically reserved for Jewish kings. This portrayal emphasizes the idea that God can use non-Israelite rulers to achieve His purposes.

The Impact on the Jewish Exiles

For the Jewish exiles, the fall of Babylon had profound implications. It meant the end of their captivity and the fulfillment of God's promise to restore them to their land. The event reinforced their belief in the God of Israel as the sovereign ruler over all nations and history.

Lessons from Babylon's Fall

The fall of Babylon teaches several lessons consistent with biblical themes:

The sovereignty of God over history and nations: Babylon's fall illustrates that God is in control of world events and rulers.

The theme of divine retribution: Babylon's downfall is seen as a just recompense for its sins and atrocities.

The impermanence of earthly power: Babylon's demise serves as a reminder that earthly kingdoms and powers are transient.

Babylon as a Symbol in Biblical Literature

In later biblical literature, particularly in the New Testament, Babylon becomes a symbol of worldly power and opposition to God. In the Book of Revelation, Babylon represents the epitome of evil, corruption, and defiance against God. Its fall, therefore, is symbolic of the ultimate victory of God's kingdom over the forces of evil.

The Restoration of Israel and Fulfillment of Prophecy

The fall of Babylon set in motion the events leading to the restoration of Israel, as prophesied by Jeremiah (Jeremiah 29:10-14). This restoration was not just physical but also spiritual, signaling a renewed covenant relationship between God and His people.

The Fall of Babylon in Salvation History

The fall of Babylon, as a fulfillment of prophecy, holds a significant place in salvation history. It exemplifies God's control over the course of human events and His faithfulness to His promises. The event stands as a powerful reminder of the transient nature of earthly powers compared to the eternal sovereignty of God. For the Jewish people, it was a time of liberation and a pivotal moment that led to their return to the Promised Land, signifying God's unwavering commitment to His covenant people and His plan of salvation.

Cyrus's Decree and the Return of the Exiles

A Monumental Edict

The decree of Cyrus the Great in 539 BCE, documented in the Bible and confirmed by archaeological findings, marks a pivotal moment in Jewish history. It signifies the end of the Babylonian Captivity and the beginning of the return to Judah, initiating a period of restoration and rebuilding.

Cyrus the Great: An Instrument of Divine Will

Cyrus, the founder of the Achaemenid Empire, is recognized in the Bible not merely as a Persian king but as an instrument of God's will. Isaiah prophetically names Cyrus as the Lord's anointed (Isaiah 44:28; 45:1), highlighting the sovereignty of God in orchestrating historical events for the fulfillment of His purposes.

The Text of Cyrus's Decree

The decree of Cyrus, as recorded in Ezra 1:1-4, allows the Jewish exiles to return to Jerusalem and rebuild the Temple. This edict is significant for several reasons:

It represents a shift in imperial policy from the assimilation practices of the Babylonians to the religious and cultural tolerance under the Persians.

The decree acknowledges the God of Israel, illustrating the influence of the Jewish community in Persia and the divine orchestration of events.

The Return of the Exiles

The response to Cyrus's decree is immediate and enthusiastic among certain segments of the Jewish population in Babylon. Led by figures such as Zerubbabel, a significant number of exiles return to Judah, enthusiastic to rebuild their homeland and their spiritual center, the Temple (Ezra 1:5-11).

Challenges in Rebuilding and Restoration

The returnees face numerous challenges in rebuilding the Temple and reestablishing their community in Judah. Opposition from neighboring peoples, logistical difficulties, and internal conflicts (Ezra 4-6) all test the resolve and faith of the returnees. These challenges underscore the complexity of restoration after a long period of exile.

Prophetic Encouragement and Guidance

Prophets like Haggai and Zechariah play crucial roles during this period, offering encouragement and guidance. Their prophetic messages focus on the importance of rebuilding the Temple as a symbol of the nation's spiritual renewal and the continuation of God's covenant promises (Haggai 1:2-8; Zechariah 1:16).

The Significance of the Temple Reconstruction

The reconstruction of the Temple, completed in 516 BCE, is not just a physical rebuilding but also a symbol of the restoration of the Jewish faith and identity. The Second Temple stands as a testament to the community's resilience and God's faithfulness to His promises.

Theological Implications of the Return

The return from exile and the events following Cyrus's decree carry profound theological implications:

They affirm the prophetic word and the trustworthiness of God's promises.

The return symbolizes a new exodus, a second deliverance for the Jewish people.

It reflects the theme of restoration and redemption, central to the biblical narrative of salvation.

Cyrus's Decree in Salvation History

Cyrus's decree and the return of the exiles are integral to salvation history. They set the stage for the re-establishment of a Jewish presence in Jerusalem, paving the way for the coming of the Messiah, as prophesied in the Old Testament.

Cyrus's Decree as a Fulcrum of Biblical History

The decree of Cyrus and the subsequent return of the Jewish exiles represent a fulcrum in biblical history. This event marks the transition from prophecy to fulfillment, from exile to restoration. It illustrates God's power to use even pagan rulers for His purposes and His commitment to redeeming and restoring His people. The return from exile, leading to the rebuilding of Jerusalem and the Temple, sets the stage for the next phase in God's redemptive plan, culminating in the arrival of Jesus Christ, the ultimate expression of God's salvation.

Rebuilding Jerusalem: Renewal of Covenant and Worship

The Significance of Rebuilding Jerusalem

The return of the Jewish exiles from Babylon and the subsequent rebuilding of Jerusalem stand as significant events in biblical history. This period marks not only a physical reconstruction of the city and the Temple but also a spiritual and communal renewal of the Jewish people.

The Return to Jerusalem

Led by figures like Zerubbabel, Ezra, and Nehemiah, the Jewish exiles begin their journey back to Jerusalem. This return fulfills the prophecy of restoration and sets the stage for the re-establishment of Jewish worship and society in their ancestral land.

The Reconstruction of the Temple

The rebuilding of the Temple, initiated by Zerubbabel, is a central aspect of this renewal (Ezra 3-6). The Temple in Jerusalem was more than a building; it was the symbolic heart of Jewish worship and national identity. Its reconstruction represents the recommitment of the Jewish people to their covenant with God and the restoration of proper worship practices.

Ezra's Leadership and Reforms

Ezra the scribe plays a pivotal role in the spiritual renewal of the people. Arriving in Jerusalem, he leads a religious revival focused on the Law of Moses. Ezra's public reading of the Law (Nehemiah 8) and his reforms are crucial in re-establishing the Law's centrality in Jewish life and worship.

Nehemiah's Role in Rebuilding the Walls

Nehemiah's contribution to the renewal of Jerusalem is marked by his leadership in rebuilding the city walls (Nehemiah 2-6). The walls symbolize not just physical protection but also the restoration of dignity and security for the Jewish community. Nehemiah's dedication to this task, despite opposition, reflects his commitment to God's work and the well-being of his people.

Challenges and Opposition

The rebuilding efforts face significant challenges, including opposition from neighboring peoples and internal social and economic issues. These challenges test the resolve of the returnees and highlight the difficulties of restoring a community after a prolonged period of dislocation and hardship.

Renewal of Covenant

A key moment in this period is the renewal of the covenant (Nehemiah 9-10). The people, led by their leaders, confess their sins and the sins of their ancestors, and recommit themselves to following God's Law. This covenant renewal ceremony is a powerful expression of repentance and rededication to God.

The Importance of Worship

The restoration of proper worship practices, including the observance of festivals like the Passover (Ezra 6:19-22), is an integral part of this renewal. Worship reconnects the community with their God and their history, serving as a vital component of their collective identity and spiritual life.

The Role of Prophecy

Prophets like Haggai and Zechariah play significant roles during this period. Their messages encourage the people in their rebuilding efforts and reaffirm God's presence and promises. These prophetic voices help the people understand their experiences within the larger framework of God's plan for His people.

Theological Significance of the Rebuilding

The rebuilding of Jerusalem and the renewal of covenant and worship carry profound theological significance:

They demonstrate God's faithfulness in restoring His people, as promised through the prophets.

The events symbolize the restoration of a broken relationship between God and His people.

They prefigure the ultimate restoration and redemption found in Jesus Christ, who establishes a new covenant through His death and resurrection.

A New Chapter in Salvation History

The end of the Babylonian exile and the rebuilding of Jerusalem mark a new chapter in the history of salvation. They represent a physical and spiritual homecoming for the Jewish people, a renewal of their covenant relationship with God, and the re-establishment of worship. This period sets the stage for the coming of the Messiah, Jesus Christ, who would fulfill the Law and the Prophets, offering salvation not just to Israel but to all humanity. The events of this era remind us of the persistent grace of God and His unending commitment to the restoration and salvation of His people.

CHAPTER 6: Atonement: Bridging the Gap Between God and Humanity

The Concept of Atonement in Biblical Theology

Understanding Atonement

Atonement, derived from the expression "at one," in biblical theology, signifies a covering or reconciliation of sins. This concept, deeply rooted in both the Hebrew Scriptures and Christian Greek Scriptures, addresses the fundamental issue of humanity's separation from God due to sin and the means by which this separation is overcome.

Atonement in the Hebrew Scriptures

In the Hebrew Scriptures, the concept of atonement is predominantly seen in the rituals and sacrifices prescribed in the Mosaic Law, especially in Leviticus and Numbers. The Hebrew word 'ka·phar'' (to cover) underlines the idea of covering or wiping off sins.

Man's Need for Atonement: Due to inherited sin from Adam, all of mankind is in need of atonement (Psalm 51:5; Romans 3:23). This inherited sin, resulting in death, requires a just and equivalent atonement to restore what was lost (Deuteronomy 19:21; Romans 5:12).

Atonement Sacrifices in Israel: Under the Mosaic Law, God instituted sacrifices as a means for the Israelites to make atonement (Leviticus 4:20). The Day of Atonement (Yom Kippur) particularly highlights the need for atonement through sacrifices. These animal sacrifices, requiring unblemished victims, pointed to the need for a perfect, corresponding sacrifice to completely atone for human sin (Hebrews 10:1-4).

Fulfillment in Christ Jesus

The Christian Greek Scriptures link Jesus Christ directly with the fulfillment of atonement. Jesus, as a sinless human, provided the perfect sacrifice, corresponding exactly to what Adam lost - perfect human life (2 Corinthians 5:21; John 1:29).

Jesus' Sacrifice as Propitiation: Jesus' sacrifice served as a propitiation, satisfying God's justice and allowing for the forgiveness of sins. This act of substitution, where Christ died for humanity, is central to the Christian understanding of atonement (1 Peter 2:24; Romans 3:25).

Reconciliation Through Christ: Sin caused a rift between humanity and God. The atonement through Christ bridges this gap, offering reconciliation to all who exercise faith in Jesus' sacrificial death (Romans 5:10-11; Ephesians 2:16).

The Cost of Atonement: The sacrificial system under the Law highlighted the costliness of atonement. Similarly, Christ's sacrifice, involving the shedding of his perfect blood, underscores the immense cost of atoning for humanity's sin (Hebrews 9:22).

Theological Implications of Atonement

Atonement carries significant theological implications in biblical theology:

Divine Justice and Mercy: The atonement reflects God's justice in requiring a penalty for sin and His mercy in providing the means for atonement through Christ.

Restoration and Redemption: Atonement is not merely about covering sins; it's about restoring the relationship between God and humanity, pointing towards ultimate redemption.

Faith and Repentance: To benefit from Christ's atonement, individuals must exhibit true repentance and faith. This requirement is consistent with the principle that mere ritual without genuine faith is inadequate (Isaiah 1:10-17).

Atonement as a Central Christian Doctrine

In Christian doctrine, atonement is central because it deals with the fundamental problem of sin and provides the only means for restoring the broken relationship with God.

It underscores the love and grace of God in making salvation possible through Jesus Christ (John 3:16; Romans 8:32).

Atonement in the Christian Faith

The doctrine of atonement is pivotal in understanding the Christian faith. It encapsulates God's plan to reconcile humanity to Himself through the sacrifice of Jesus Christ, addressing the consequences of sin and offering redemption and eternal life. This doctrine highlights the gravity of sin, the holiness of God, the necessity of divine justice, and the unparalleled love and mercy of God in providing a means for salvation.

Old Testament Sacrificial System: Foreshadowing Christ's Sacrifice

The Foundation of Atonement in the Old Testament

The concept of atonement in the Old Testament is deeply rooted in the sacrificial system established under the Mosaic Law. This system, with its detailed rituals and offerings, serves as a profound foreshadowing of the ultimate sacrifice of Christ, which provides the complete atonement for humanity's sins.

The Nature of Atonement in the Mosaic Law

The Hebrew Concept of Atonement: The Hebrew term 'ka·phar', often translated as "atone" or "cover," conveys the idea of covering sins. This concept is central to the Old Testament's understanding of how humanity can achieve reconciliation with God.

Sacrificial System as a Means of Atonement: The sacrificial system, particularly detailed in Leviticus, provided a means for the Israelites to approach God despite their sins. The offerings, especially on the Day of Atonement (Yom Kippur), were central to this system (Leviticus 16).

The Day of Atonement: A Central Component

Rituals and Significance: The Day of Atonement involved intricate rituals performed by the high priest. This day was the culmination of Israel's sacrificial system, providing annual atonement for the sins of the priests and the people.

Symbolism of Sacrifices: The unblemished animals used in these sacrifices symbolized the need for a perfect, sinless offering to fully atone for sin. The act of transferring sins to the animal and its subsequent death symbolized the removal of sin and the restoration of the relationship with God.

The Limitations of Animal Sacrifices

Temporary and Symbolic Nature: The animal sacrifices were temporary and could not fully remove sin

(Hebrews 10:1-4). They served as symbols, pointing to the need for a greater, more perfect sacrifice.

The Inadequacy of Animals Compared to Humans: Since animals are inferior to humans, their sacrifice could not completely cover human sin, highlighting the need for a human equivalent to atone for human sin.

Fulfillment in Christ Jesus

Christ as the Antitypical Sacrifice: Jesus Christ, in the New Testament, is presented as the fulfillment of these Old Testament types and symbols. As a perfect human, He provided the exact atonement required to cover Adam's sin and its consequences.

The Superiority of Christ's Sacrifice: Unlike the repeated animal sacrifices, Christ's sacrifice was once for all (Hebrews 10:12). His offering was not only sufficient to cover sins but also to remove them entirely.

The Sacrificial System Pointing to Christ

Prophetic Foreshadowing: The sacrificial system, in its complexity and detail, served as a prophetic foreshadowing of Christ's work. Each aspect, from the selection of the animal to the role of the high priest, was a type of the work Christ would accomplish.

Teaching the Cost of Sin: The sacrificial system taught the Israelites about the severity of sin and the cost of atonement. It was a constant reminder of humanity's need for redemption.

Reconciliation Through Christ

Bridging the Gap: The sacrificial system highlighted the chasm sin created between humanity and God. Christ's sacrifice bridges this gap, offering complete reconciliation with God (Romans 5:11).

A New Covenant in Christ: Christ's sacrifice inaugurated a new covenant, fulfilling the law and the prophets (Matthew 5:17). This new covenant offers a deeper, more intimate relationship with God, based on the complete atonement provided by Christ.

Understanding Atonement Through the Old Testament Lens

The Old Testament sacrificial system is crucial in understanding the full significance of Christ's atonement. It provided a framework through which the Israelites understood their sin and need for redemption. In Christ, these symbols and rituals find their fulfillment, offering a complete, once-for-all atonement for humanity. This atonement is not merely a covering of sins but their total eradication, thereby restoring the broken relationship between God and humanity. Through this lens, the depth of God's love and the magnitude of Christ's sacrifice are profoundly appreciated, highlighting the central place of atonement in Christian faith and theology.

The Day of Atonement: Symbolism and Significance

The Day of Atonement in Biblical Context

The Day of Atonement, or Yom Kippur, stands as a central observance in the Old Testament, particularly within the Mosaic Law. It was a day of solemnity and profound significance, symbolizing the atonement of sins for the people of Israel and foreshadowing the redemptive work of Jesus Christ.

Historical and Ritualistic Background

Time and Observance: Celebrated on the tenth day of the seventh month (Tishri), the Day of Atonement was a unique annual event in the Israelite religious calendar, marked by fasting, rest, and solemn reflection (Leviticus 16:29-31).

High Priest's Central Role: The high priest played a crucial role, performing intricate rituals that symbolized the atonement of sins. This included entering the Most Holy Place of the tabernacle or temple, an act reserved solely for this occasion (Hebrews 9:7; Leviticus 16:2, 12, 14-15).

The Symbolism of the Rituals

Sacrifices and Offerings: The high priest offered a bull for his own sins and goats for the sins of the people. These sacrifices highlighted the seriousness of sin and the need for atonement.

The Scapegoat Ritual: One of the two goats, chosen by lot, was designated as the scapegoat (Azazel) and symbolically bore the sins of the people, being sent into the wilderness (Leviticus 16:8-10, 20-22).

The Significance of Blood: The blood of the sacrificed animals, sprinkled in the Most Holy Place, signified the life given for atonement and the sanctification of the sacred space from the defilement of sin (Leviticus 17:11).

The Need for a Perfect Sacrifice: The requirement for unblemished sacrificial animals indicated the necessity for a perfect, sinless atonement. This pointed forward to the need for a perfect human sacrifice to atone for sin effectively.

The Day of Atonement and Its Limitations

A Shadow of Good Things to Come: The repeated annual observance of the Day of Atonement underscored its temporary and symbolic nature, pointing to the need for a more permanent solution to the problem of sin (Hebrews 10:1-4).

The Inability of Animal Sacrifices: The use of animals for sacrifices, while ordained by God, could not ultimately remove the burden of sin, underscoring the limitations of the sacrificial system (Hebrews 10:4).

Fulfillment in Christ

Christ as the Antitypical High Priest: Jesus Christ is presented in the New Testament as the ultimate High Priest, who entered not a man-made sanctuary, but heaven itself, offering not the blood of animals, but His own blood (Hebrews 9:11-12, 24-28).

The Once-for-All Sacrifice: Unlike the repeated sacrifices of the Old Testament, Christ's sacrifice was once for all, effectively dealing with sin and opening a new way of access to God (Hebrews 9:26-28).

Theological Implications

God's Holiness and Justice: The Day of Atonement emphasized God's absolute holiness and the seriousness with which He regards sin, requiring atonement for reconciliation.

Grace and Mercy: Simultaneously, it highlighted God's mercy and grace, providing a means for the atonement of sins and the maintenance of the covenant relationship.

Personal Repentance and Faith: The individual response of 'afflicting one's soul' symbolized repentance and humility, a necessary attitude for forgiveness and reconciliation with God.

The Enduring Significance of the Day of Atonement

The Day of Atonement in the Old Testament holds enduring significance in Christian theology. It vividly illustrates humanity's need for redemption and God's provision for atonement through the sacrificial system, which finds its ultimate fulfillment in the sacrifice of Jesus Christ. This observance serves as a profound reminder of the cost of sin, the necessity of a sacrificial atonement, and the depth of God's love and grace in providing the ultimate means of reconciliation for humanity.

The Fulfillment of Atonement in Christ's Sacrifice

The Significance of Christ's Sacrifice

The concept of atonement reaches its climax in the New Testament with the sacrifice of Jesus Christ. This fulfillment not only transcends but also completes the Old Testament sacrificial system, offering a permanent solution to the problem of sin and separation from God.

The Need for a Perfect Atonement

Humanity's Sin and Its Consequences: Inherited sin from Adam brought about spiritual death and separation from God (Romans 5:12; Psalm 51:5). This created an absolute necessity for a perfect atonement that could bridge this gap.

The Limitation of the Law: The Mosaic Law, with its sacrificial system, was incapable of providing a lasting solution to sin. Its offerings were symbolic and pointed towards a need for a greater sacrifice (Hebrews 10:1-4).

Christ: The Antitypical Sacrifice

Fulfillment of Old Testament Prophecies: Jesus Christ, as the Messiah, fulfilled the prophetic types and shadows of the Old Testament. His sacrifice corresponded exactly to what was symbolized in the Law (Isaiah 53:7; John 1:29).

The Unblemished Lamb: Christ, being sinless, was the perfect sacrifice, contrasting with the imperfect animal sacrifices of the Old Covenant (1 Peter 2:22; Hebrews 9:14).

The Sacrificial Work of Christ

The Propitiation for Sins: Jesus' death served as a propitiation, satisfying God's justice and turning away His wrath from humanity (1 John 4:10; Hebrews 2:17).

Redemption Through His Blood: The shedding of Christ's blood was crucial for the remission of sins, fulfilling the legal requirement of blood for atonement (Hebrews 9:22; Ephesians 1:7).

The Role of Substitution: Christ's sacrifice was substitutionary; He bore the sins of humanity in His body, providing a way for reconciliation with God (2 Corinthians 5:21; 1 Peter 2:24).

The Effects of Christ's Atonement

Reconciliation with God: Through Christ's sacrifice, the breach caused by sin is healed, allowing humans to have a restored relationship with God (Romans 5:10-11).

Eternal Redemption: Unlike the temporary atonement of the Old Testament, Christ's sacrifice offers eternal redemption, securing an everlasting inheritance for believers (Hebrews 9:12).

A New Covenant in His Blood: Jesus' death inaugurated a new covenant, replacing the old covenant and its sacrificial system (Luke 22:20; Hebrews 8:6-13).

Personal Application of the Atonement

Faith and Repentance: To benefit from Christ's atonement, individuals must respond in faith and repentance, recognizing their need for His redemptive work (Acts 4:12; Hebrews 10:26-31).

Living a Life of Righteousness: Christ's atonement not only provides forgiveness but also empowers believers to live righteously, being transformed by His grace (Titus 2:11-14; 1 Peter 2:24).

The Comprehensive Scope of Christ's Atonement

The fulfillment of atonement in Christ's sacrifice is central to Christian theology. It encapsulates God's love and justice, providing a comprehensive solution to the problem of sin and death. This sacrifice stands as the ultimate expression of God's mercy, offering humanity not just a covering for sins, but complete redemption and restoration. Through Christ, believers are not only reconciled to God but are also called to a life of holiness and service, reflecting the transformative power of His atoning work.

Atonement and the Believer: Implications for Christian Life

The Personal Impact of Atonement

Atonement in Christ is not just a theological concept but a transformative reality that shapes the Christian life. Understanding the profound implications of atonement helps believers live in a way that honors the sacrificial love of Christ and deepens their relationship with God.

Understanding the Depth of Atonement

Recognition of Sin and Grace: Atonement begins with the acknowledgment of one's sinful nature, inherited from Adam, and the recognition of the grace provided through Christ's sacrifice (Romans 5:12; Ephesians 2:8-9).

The Cost of Forgiveness: Realizing the depth of Christ's suffering for humanity's sin fosters a profound sense of gratitude and humility, acknowledging the high price paid for redemption (1 Peter 2:24; Isaiah 53:5).

The Transformative Power of Atonement

New Life in Christ: Atonement brings about a new spiritual birth, transforming believers from a state of sin to a new life in Christ (2 Corinthians 5:17; Romans 6:4).

Freedom from Guilt and Condemnation: Christ's atoning sacrifice removes the burden of guilt and the condemnation of sin, granting believers the freedom to live a life dedicated to God (Romans 8:1; Hebrews 10:22).

Living a Life of Faith and Obedience

Faith as the Response: Embracing atonement requires faith, a trust in Christ's work and a commitment to live according to His teachings (John 3:16; Ephesians 2:8).

Obedience to God's Will: Understanding the atonement leads to a desire to obey God's commandments, not as a means of earning salvation, but as an expression of love and gratitude (1 John 5:3; James 2:18).

Holiness and Sanctification

Called to Holiness: Believers are called to live in holiness, reflecting the nature of God in their lives, a process enabled by the atoning work of Christ (1 Peter 1:15-16; Ephesians 4:24).

Ongoing Sanctification: Atonement is not a one-time event but an ongoing process of sanctification, where believers continually grow in Christlikeness (Philippians 2:12-13; 1 Thessalonians 4:3).

Communion with God and the Church

Restored Relationship with God: Atonement restores the relationship between God and humanity, allowing for intimate communion with God through prayer, worship, and the study of Scripture (John 17:3; Hebrews 4:16).

Community and Fellowship: Believers are called into a community, the church, where they can experience fellowship, accountability, and mutual encouragement (Hebrews 10:24-25; 1 Corinthians 12:12-27).

Moral and Ethical Implications

Living Righteously: Atonement calls believers to live a life that reflects the righteousness of Christ, impacting their moral and ethical decisions (Ephesians 4:1; Titus 2:12).

Witnessing to the World: The life of a believer, transformed by atonement, serves as a testimony to the redemptive power of Christ to the world (Matthew 5:16; 1 Peter 3:15).

Embracing Atonement in Daily Life

Atonement through Christ is foundational to the Christian faith, affecting every aspect of a believer's life. It calls for a response of faith, leading to a transformed life marked by holiness, obedience, and active participation in the community of believers. Living under the reality of atonement involves continual growth in grace, a deeper communion with God, and a commitment to reflecting Christ's love and righteousness in the world. This understanding of atonement empowers believers to live a life that truly glorifies God and spreads the message of His redemptive love.

CHAPTER 7: Ransom: The Cost of Redemption

Understanding Ransom in Biblical Context

The Concept of Ransom

The term "ransom" is pivotal in understanding the scriptural theme of redemption. It signifies a price paid to recover something or someone. This concept is extensively woven into the fabric of the Bible, providing a profound understanding of God's plan for humanity's salvation through Christ Jesus.

Old Testament Foundations of Ransom

Hebrew Terms and Their Significance: The Hebrew word for ransom, *ko'pher*, derives from *ka·phar'*, meaning "to cover," indicating the price or means of atonement. The Old Testament uses various terms to express the idea of redemption and ransom, each underscoring the notion of a price paid for release or recovery.

Sacrificial System as a Precursor: The Mosaic Law instituted sacrifices as a means for atoning sin. These offerings, though symbolic, pointed to the need for a greater, more effective ransom—a perfect sacrifice for humanity's sin.

Ransom in the New Testament

Fulfillment in Christ Jesus: The New Testament reveals that the true and complete ransom was provided by Jesus Christ. His perfect, sinless life, offered in sacrifice, was the only effective counterbalance for the sin and imperfection introduced by Adam.

Christ's Sacrifice as a Corresponding Ransom: Jesus, the "last Adam," provided what Adam lost—perfect human life. This act of atonement was not merely a general sacrifice but a corresponding ransom, specific and equivalent, fulfilling the divine justice requirements.

Implications of the Ransom for Humanity

Universal Provision, Individual Acceptance: While the ransom sacrifice of Christ is universally available, it requires individual acceptance. It brings about reconciliation with God, delivering mankind from the inherited sin and death from Adam.

Ransom and Salvation: The ransom is fundamental to Christian salvation. It is the mechanism through which forgiveness of sins, reconciliation with God, and the hope of eternal life are made possible.

Practical Aspects of Ransom in Christian Living

Motivation for Righteous Living: The realization of the ransom price paid for their sin moves Christians to live a life of gratitude, holiness, and godly devotion.

Evangelism and Witnessing: The knowledge of Christ's ransom sacrifice compels believers to share this good news with others, fulfilling the Great Commission.

Ransom in Eschatological Context

Role in God's Kingdom Purpose: The ransom sacrifice is central to the fulfillment of God's Kingdom purpose. It not only redeems mankind from sin but also restores the original purpose of God for humanity and the earth.

Hope for the Future: The ransom ensures the resurrection hope, the promise of a new earth where righteousness dwells, and the ultimate restoration of perfect human life.

The Centrality of Ransom in Christian Doctrine

The doctrine of ransom is not merely a theological concept but the very heart of Christian faith. It defines the depth of God's love and justice, showcases the perfect obedience of Christ, and offers every believer a solid foundation for hope and eternal life. Understanding ransom in its biblical context is essential for appreciating the magnitude of what God has accomplished through Christ, motivating believers to live in a way that honors this profound gift.

Ransom Imagery in the Old Testament

The Concept of Ransom in the Old Testament

In the Hebrew Scriptures, the concept of ransom is deeply rooted and multifaceted, reflecting the justice, mercy, and redemptive purpose of Jehovah. The idea of a ransom—a price paid to release or redeem—is intricately linked to the divine plan for humanity's salvation.

Key Hebrew Terms and Their Meanings

Ka·phar' and *ko'pher*: These terms, meaning "to cover" and "the price for atonement" respectively, are central in understanding Old Testament ransom imagery. They depict the process of covering or atoning for sins, symbolically through sacrifices, pointing toward a greater fulfillment.

Pa·dhah' and *pidh·yohn'*: These words emphasize the act of releasing or redemption, often used in contexts of deliverance from slavery or distress. They highlight the aspect of liberation associated with the ransom.

Ga·'al' and *go·'el'*: These terms relate to the rights of redemption and reclaiming, often in the context of a kinsman-redeemer. They stress the familial and relational aspect of redemption.

Sacrificial System as a Type of Christ's Sacrifice

The sacrificial system under the Mosaic Law serves as a shadow of the greater sacrifice of Christ. The offerings, particularly on the Day of Atonement, symbolize the need for a perfect ransom to atone for humanity's sins fully and effectively.

Legal and Social Applications of Ransom

The law concerning the goring bull (Exodus 21:28-32) illustrates the principle of a ransom or compensation in legal matters, emphasizing the need for justice to be satisfied.

The provision for redeeming land, property, or individuals (Leviticus 25) underlines the importance of redemption in maintaining social and familial stability and points to the role of the Messiah as the ultimate Redeemer.

Prophetic Foreshadowing of the Messiah as Redeemer

The role of the kinsman-redeemer, as exemplified in the story of Ruth, foreshadows the coming of Christ, who would redeem humanity not just from physical bondage but from spiritual slavery.

The prophets, particularly Isaiah, speak of God redeeming His people from exile, symbolizing the greater redemption from sin and death that would be accomplished by the Messiah.

Personal Applications of Redemption

Figures like Job (Job 19:25) express confidence in a Redeemer, indicating an understanding of personal salvation and redemption beyond the immediate physical context.

Transition to the New Testament Fulfillment

The Old Testament ransom imagery sets the stage for the New Testament fulfillment in Christ. It provides a framework for understanding the significance of Jesus' sacrifice as the true ransom that covers sin, liberates from bondage, and restores relationship with God.

The Old Testament's rich imagery of ransom lays a foundational understanding of God's redemptive plan. It foreshadows the coming of Christ, whose sacrifice fulfills these types and shadows, offering a perfect, once-for-all ransom for humanity's sin. This deep-rooted concept in the Hebrew Scriptures enhances the appreciation of the magnitude of Christ's sacrificial role as the ultimate Redeemer and Ransomer.

Jesus Christ: The Ransom for Many

The Concept of Ransom

The concept of ransom is central to Christian doctrine, particularly in understanding the role of Jesus Christ in God's plan of salvation. Ransom, as used Biblically, refers to the price paid to redeem or buy back humanity from sin and death. The most significant expression of this is found in the sacrifice of Jesus Christ.

The Ransom in the Old Testament Context

Foundation in the Hebrew Scriptures: The idea of ransom in the Old Testament is deeply ingrained in the sacrificial system and the legal code of Israel. The terms *ka·phar'* (to cover) and *ko'pher* (ransom price) illustrate the necessity of a covering for sins.

Sacrificial System as a Precursor: The Old Testament sacrifices, particularly on the Day of Atonement, symbolized the need for a substantial ransom to fully atone for humanity's sin.

Legal Aspects of Ransom: Instances such as the law concerning the goring bull demonstrate the concept of a ransom as a means to satisfy justice, highlighting the principle of life for life.

Jesus Christ: The Fulfillment of the Ransom

The Need for a Perfect Ransom: Under the Mosaic Law, animal sacrifices served as a temporary covering for sins. However, they were insufficient for complete atonement. Christ's sacrifice, being perfect and sinless, was the only offering capable of fully redeeming humanity.

The Incarnation: Jesus, born of the virgin Mary and overshadowed by God's spirit, was free from inherited sin. This sinlessness qualified him to be the perfect ransom.

Christ's Sacrificial Death: Jesus' willing sacrifice on the cross, shedding his blood, was the actualization of the ransom. His death fulfilled the legal requirements set forth in the Scriptures, offering redemption for Adam's descendants.

Scriptural Affirmations: New Testament passages affirm that Christ's death was a ransom for many, a theme emphasized in texts like Matthew 20:28, Mark 10:45, and 1 Timothy 2:5-6. The Greek terms used in these contexts (*ly'tron*, *an·ti'ly·tron*) underline the idea of a corresponding price, a substitutionary sacrifice.

The Effectiveness and Scope of Christ's Ransom

Universal Offer, Selective Acceptance: While Christ's ransom is available to all, it is effective only for those who accept it. This acceptance involves faith, repentance, and adherence to God's commandments.

Redemption Beyond Legalism: Christ's ransom transcends the legal framework of the Mosaic Law, offering a relational redemption that restores the broken relationship between humanity and God.

Christ as the Second Adam: Jesus is often referred to as the "last Adam" (1 Corinthians 15:45), indicating that his sacrifice counteracts the effects of the first Adam's sin, offering life where there was death.

Implications for Christian Believers

A New Covenant Relationship: Believers enter into a new covenant with God through Christ's ransom, ensuring their salvation and hope of eternal life.

Ethical and Moral Transformation: The acceptance of Christ's ransom leads to a transformation in believers' lives, guiding them to live in a way that reflects their redeemed status.

Hope of Resurrection and Eternal Life: The ransom assures believers of the resurrection and the promise of eternal life, fulfilling the prophetic visions of the Old Testament and the teachings of Christ.

The Ransom as God's Supreme Act of Love

Jesus Christ's role as the ransom for many is the pinnacle of God's redemptive plan. It demonstrates God's justice, mercy, and love in a profound way, offering humanity a way back to Him through Christ's sacrificial death and resurrection. This doctrine remains a cornerstone of Christian faith, emphasizing the depth of God's love and the transformative power of Christ's sacrifice.

Theological Significance of Christ as a Ransom

The Concept of Ransom in Christian Theology

The idea of ransom is deeply embedded in Christian theology, representing the price paid to redeem humanity from sin and death. This concept is intricately linked to the redemptive work of Jesus Christ, whose sacrifice is viewed as the ultimate ransom.

Ransom in the Old Testament: Foreshadowing the Christ

Old Testament Foundations: The Old Testament (Hebrew Scriptures) lays the groundwork for the concept of ransom. The Hebrew terms *ka·phar'* (to cover) and *ko'pher* (ransom price) provide a basis for understanding the sacrificial system as a precursor to the ultimate ransom by Christ.

Sacrificial Precedents: The sacrificial rituals, especially the Day of Atonement, were symbolic representations of the need for a significant ransom to atone for humanity's sins. These sacrifices, while covering sins, pointed to a greater need that could only be fulfilled by the Messiah.

Legal and Ethical Implications: The legal framework within the Mosaic Law, such as the redemption of a life for a life, underscores the gravity of sin and the necessity of a corresponding price for redemption.

The Ransom Paid by Jesus Christ

The Perfect Sacrifice: Unlike the animal sacrifices of the Old Testament, which were temporary and insufficient, Christ's sacrifice was perfect and complete. His sinless nature, affirmed in the New Testament, made Him the only viable option for a true atonement for sin.

The Incarnation and Sacrifice: The incarnation of Jesus Christ — His birth as a human, free from inherited sin — set the stage for the ultimate ransom. His death on the cross, where He shed His blood, was the fulfillment of the Old Testament types and prophecies.

Biblical Affirmations of the Ransom: New Testament scriptures reinforce the idea of Christ's death as a ransom. Terms like *ly'tron* and *an·ti'ly·tron* are used to describe His sacrificial role, emphasizing the substitutionary nature of His death.

The Effectiveness of Christ's Ransom

Salvation Through Ransom: The sacrifice of Christ opened the way for salvation to all who accept it. This acceptance is marked by faith, repentance, and a commitment to live according to God's will.

Beyond Legalism to Relationship: Christ's ransom transcends the legalistic framework of the Mosaic Law, offering a restored relationship with God and the promise of eternal life.

Christ as the Last Adam: Christ is often referred to as the "last Adam," signifying that His death and resurrection reverse the effects of the first Adam's sin, bringing life instead of death.

Implications for Christian Belief and Practice

A New Covenant: Believers in Christ enter into a new covenant relationship with God, secured by the ransom paid by Christ. This assures them of salvation and eternal life.

Ethical and Moral Transformation: Embracing Christ's ransom leads to a moral and ethical transformation, guiding believers to live in a manner befitting their redeemed status.

Hope and Assurance: The ransom provides believers with the hope of resurrection and the assurance of eternal life, fulfilling both Old Testament prophecies and Christ's teachings.

The Ransom as a Manifestation of Divine Love and Justice

The ransom provided by Jesus Christ is the pinnacle of God's redemptive plan, demonstrating His justice and mercy. It underscores the depth of God's love and the transformative power of Christ's sacrifice, making it a central pillar of Christian faith. This doctrine highlights the reconciliation between God and humanity, offering a pathway to salvation and eternal life through the sacrificial death and resurrection of Christ.

Ransom and Christian Discipleship: Application and Response

The Significance of Ransom in Christian Discipleship

The doctrine of the ransom paid by Jesus Christ has profound implications for Christian discipleship. It is not just a theological concept but a transformative truth that demands a response and shapes the life of a believer.

Understanding the Ransom

The Nature of the Ransom: As previously outlined, the ransom is the price paid by Jesus Christ to redeem humanity from sin and death. This understanding is rooted in the satisfaction of divine justice, where Christ's sacrificial death covers (ka·phar′) the sin of humanity, fulfilling the Old Testament types and prophecies.

The Exchange Involved: The ransom involves an exchange – the sinless life of Christ for the sinful lives of humanity. This exchange underscores the immense value of Christ's sacrifice and the depth of God's love for mankind.

Response to the Ransom in Christian Life

Faith and Acceptance: The primary response to Christ's ransom is faith. Believers are called to trust in the efficacy of Christ's sacrifice for their salvation. This faith is not merely intellectual assent but a heartfelt reliance on Christ's atoning work.

Repentance and Transformation: Accepting the ransom involves turning away from sin. It is a call to a transformed life, where the believer strives to live in a way that honors the sacrifice made for their redemption.

Baptism and Public Declaration: Baptism serves as a public declaration of one's faith in Christ's ransom and signifies the believer's death to their old life of sin and resurrection to a new life in Christ.

Living Out the Ransom in Daily Life

Holiness and Sanctification: The ransom calls believers to a life of holiness and sanctification. Understanding the price paid for their redemption motivates Christians to live in a way that reflects the holiness of God.

Service and Ministry: The ransom also compels believers to engage in service and ministry, sharing the good news of Christ's sacrifice with others and serving the needy and marginalized as an expression of Christ's love.

Endurance and Hope: The ransom instills hope and endurance, enabling believers to persevere through trials and tribulations, knowing that their redemption has been secured at a great price.

Communal and Ecclesiastical Implications

The Church as a Redeemed Community: The church, as a community of believers, is a direct result of Christ's ransom. It is a community called to live out the redemptive implications of the ransom in fellowship, worship, and mutual edification.

Worship and Sacraments: Worship and sacraments (like the Lord's Supper) in the church are a celebration and remembrance of Christ's ransom. These practices nurture the believer's faith and reinforce the reality of redemption.

Ethical Living and Social Justice: The church is also called to ethical living and the pursuit of social justice, reflecting Christ's redemptive work not just spiritually but also in societal structures and relationships.

Ransom as the Foundation of Christian Discipleship

The ransom paid by Christ is not merely a foundational doctrine but the very heartbeat of Christian discipleship. It calls for a profound response – a life lived in faith, holiness, service, and hope. The understanding of Christ as the ransom should permeate every aspect of a believer's life, shaping their identity, conduct, and mission. This doctrine, thus, stands as a constant reminder of the cost of redemption and the grace that flows from Christ's sacrificial love.

Edward D. Andrews

CHAPTER 8: Reconciliation: Restoring Broken Relationships

The Need for Reconciliation: Human Sinfulness and Separation from God

Reconciliation with God is a fundamental theme in Christian theology, focusing on restoring the broken relationship between humans and their Creator. This need arises from the inherent sinfulness of humanity, which has led to a profound separation from God.

Human Sinfulness and Its Consequences

Origin of Sin: The Bible attributes the origin of human sinfulness to the first man, Adam. His disobedience introduced sin into the human race, resulting in both physical and spiritual death (Romans 5:12). This inherited sin nature has permeated every aspect of human existence, alienating humanity from a holy God.

The Nature of Sin: Sin is more than just wrong actions; it is a state of being that opposes God's nature and laws. The inherent sinfulness of humanity leads to actions that violate God's perfect standards, creating a barrier between humans and God (Psalm 5:4; Isaiah 43:27).

The Consequences of Sin: The primary consequence of sin is spiritual death, which is eternal separation from God (Romans 6:23). This separation impacts all aspects of human life, leading to a broken world characterized by suffering, injustice, and mortality.

The Necessity of Reconciliation

Divine Holiness and Justice: God's holiness and justice demand a response to sin. He cannot simply overlook or condone sin, as doing so would compromise His nature (Psalm 89:14; Hebrews 1:9).

God's Righteous Standard: God's standard of righteousness is perfection, which humans cannot attain due to their sinful nature (Isaiah 64:6; Romans 3:23). This creates an insurmountable gap between humans and God.

The Need for a Mediator: Due to the gravity of human sin and the holiness of God, a mediator is necessary to bridge the gap. This mediator must be able to satisfy God's justice and provide a way for humans to be restored to a right relationship with God.

The Basis for Reconciliation: Christ's Sacrifice

Christ as the Propitiation: Jesus Christ's sacrificial death on the cross serves as the propitiation for human sin (1 John 2:2; 4:10). Propitiation means that Christ's death satisfied the demands of God's justice, allowing God to forgive sin without compromising His righteousness.

The Exchange at the Cross: On the cross, Jesus exchanged His righteousness for human sinfulness (2 Corinthians 5:21). He took the punishment that humans deserved, providing the basis for their reconciliation with God.

The Offer of Grace: Through Christ's sacrifice, God offers grace to sinful humanity. This grace is not cheap or easy; it cost God His Son. However, it is offered freely to all who would accept it, allowing them to be reconciled to God (Ephesians 2:8-9).

The Process of Reconciliation

Recognition of Sin and Repentance: The first step towards reconciliation is acknowledging one's sinfulness and the need for God's grace. True repentance involves a change of heart and mind, turning away from sin and towards God.

Faith in Christ: Reconciliation with God is possible through faith in Jesus Christ and His atoning work on the cross (John 14:6; Romans 5:1). This faith is more than intellectual assent; it is a trust in Christ as Lord and Savior.

The New Relationship: Once reconciled, believers enter into a new relationship with God. They are no longer enemies of God but are adopted as His children (John 1:12;

Romans 8:15-17). This relationship is characterized by love, intimacy, and ongoing transformation into the likeness of Christ.

Reconciliation with God is central to the Christian faith. It addresses the fundamental problem of human sinfulness and provides the only solution through the sacrificial death of Jesus Christ. This restored relationship with God is the foundation for a transformed life and the ultimate hope for eternity with God.

Reconciliation in the Old Testament: Prophetic Promises

The concept of reconciliation, as portrayed in the Old Testament, is deeply intertwined with the prophetic promises and God's plan for restoring harmony between Himself and humanity. This chapter delves into how these promises foreshadow the ultimate reconciliation achieved through Christ, as highlighted in the New Testament.

Prophetic Foundations of Reconciliation

The Old Testament prophets, acting as God's mouthpieces, laid the foundation for understanding reconciliation. They spoke of a future where God would restore His relationship with humanity, which had been marred by sin and disobedience.

The Promise of a New Covenant

The prophetic promise of a new covenant is central to understanding reconciliation in the Old Testament. This is vividly illustrated in Jeremiah 31:31-34, where God promises a new covenant, different from the one He made with the ancestors of Israel. This covenant would be characterized by God's laws being written on the hearts of His people, and a deeper, more intimate knowledge of Jehovah.

Isaiah's Servant Songs

Isaiah's Servant Songs (Isaiah 42:1-9, 49:1-7, 50:4-11, 52:13-53:12) depict a suffering servant who plays a crucial role in reconciling God and humanity. This servant, understood by Christians as a prophecy about Jesus Christ, would bear the iniquities of many and intercede for sinners, thus bridging the gap between a holy God and a sinful people.

The Role of Sacrifice in Reconciliation

Sacrifice is a key theme in the Old Testament's concept of reconciliation. The sacrificial system, as outlined in Leviticus, was a means by which the Israelites could atone for their sins and restore their relationship with God. This system pointed towards the ultimate sacrifice of Christ, who would offer Himself once and for all for the sins of humanity.

The Prophets' Call to Repentance

The prophets consistently called the people to repentance, highlighting that reconciliation with God required turning away from sin and returning to Him. This theme is evident in the ministries of prophets like Hosea and Joel, who urged Israel to return to Jehovah with all their hearts (Joel 2:12-13).

Illustrations of Reconciliation

The Old Testament narratives often illustrate the principle of reconciliation. The story of Joseph and his brothers (Genesis 37-50) is a powerful example of reconciliation among humans, which also reflects God's desire to reconcile with His people.

The Hope of Restoration

The prophets also spoke of a time of restoration, where God would gather His scattered people and renew their fortunes. This restoration was not just physical but also spiritual, symbolizing the ultimate reconciliation through the Messiah.

In conclusion, the Old Testament's concept of reconciliation is rich and multifaceted, rooted in the prophetic promises of a new covenant, the role of sacrifice, the call to repentance, illustrative narratives, and the hope of restoration. These elements collectively point towards the ultimate reconciliation achieved through Jesus Christ, as revealed in the New Testament.

This understanding of reconciliation aligns with the biblical, literal interpretation of the Bible, underscoring that God's plan for reconciliation was not an afterthought but a well-orchestrated design woven through the tapestry of Scripture from Genesis to Revelation. As such, the Old Testament's teachings on reconciliation are not only historically and theologically significant but also serve as a precursor to the profound realization of this doctrine in the person and work of Jesus Christ.

Edward D. Andrews

The Ministry of Reconciliation through Christ

In Christian theology, the ministry of reconciliation through Christ is a fundamental doctrine that illustrates how Jesus Christ, through His sacrifice, bridged the chasm caused by sin between God and humanity. This reconciliation, pivotal to the doctrine of salvation, entails a profound transformation of the relationship between the Creator and His creation.

The Need for Reconciliation

The biblical narrative from Genesis onwards describes the estrangement between God and humanity due to sin. This separation necessitated an intervention for reconciliation, as God, in His holiness, cannot condone sin. The Old Testament, with its sacrificial system, foreshadowed the need for a more permanent solution.

Christ's Role in Reconciliation

Jesus Christ, through His life, death, and resurrection, fulfilled this need for an eternal sacrifice. His death on the cross is seen as the pivotal event in reconciling humanity to God. As Paul states in Romans 5:10, "For if, when we were enemies, we were reconciled to God by the death of His Son, much more, being reconciled, we shall be saved by His life."

Atonement through the Cross

The cross of Christ is central to this reconciliation. It was through His suffering and death that the penalty for sin was paid, satisfying the demands of divine justice. This atonement (at-one-ment) brought humanity and God back into a harmonious relationship.

Christ as Mediator

Christ serves as the mediator between God and man. As 1 Timothy 2:5 states, "For there is one God, and one mediator between God and men, the man Christ Jesus." His unique position as fully God and fully man enables Him to bridge the gap between the two parties.

The Concept of Imputed Righteousness

In the process of reconciliation, there is a transfer or imputation of righteousness. Believers are seen as righteous in God's eyes, not because of their own merit, but because of the righteousness of Christ imputed to them through faith. This is a core principle in Pauline theology, particularly in Romans and Galatians.

The Ministry of Reconciliation

Paul describes the ministry of reconciliation as a key responsibility of the Christian church. In 2 Corinthians 5:18-19, he writes, "All this is from God, who reconciled us to himself through Christ and gave us the ministry of reconciliation." This ministry involves proclaiming the message of reconciliation to the world.

Ambassadors for Christ

Believers are called to be ambassadors for Christ, as though God were making His appeal through them. This ambassadorial role involves spreading the gospel and imploring others on Christ's behalf to be reconciled to God.

Reconciliation and the Church

The church, as the body of Christ, plays a crucial role in this ministry. It is through the church that the message of reconciliation is proclaimed and lived out. The church's unity and love are a testimony to the power of reconciliation through Christ.

In summary, the ministry of reconciliation through Christ is a central theme of Christian doctrine, emphasizing the work of Christ in reconciling a fallen humanity to a holy God. This reconciliation is not only a restoration of relationship but also an impartation of righteousness to believers, making them fit for communion with God. The church's role in this process is to continue Christ's ministry on earth, proclaiming and living out the message of reconciliation. This doctrine holds a significant place in the biblical, literal interpretation of Scripture, focusing on the redemptive work of Christ as the only means of restoring the broken relationship between God and man.

The Role of the Church in the Ministry of Reconciliation

In Christian doctrine, the church plays a crucial role in the ministry of reconciliation, as established by Christ and articulated by the apostle Paul. This ministry is rooted in the fundamental belief that through Jesus Christ's sacrifice, humanity is offered reconciliation with God, overcoming the alienation caused by sin. The church's mission, therefore, is to facilitate this reconciliation both within its community and in its outreach to the world.

Understanding the Church's Role

1. **Proclamation of the Gospel**:

The primary role of the church in the ministry of reconciliation is to proclaim the Gospel of Jesus Christ. This message centers on the death and resurrection of Christ, which provides the means for reconciliation between God and man. The church communicates this message through preaching, teaching, and personal evangelism, emphasizing that reconciliation with God is available to all through faith in Jesus Christ (2 Corinthians 5:19-20).

2. **Living as Reconciled Community**:

The church is called to be a living example of reconciliation. This involves fostering a community where barriers of sin, hostility, and division are broken down through Christ's love. The unity and love demonstrated within the church serve as a witness to the power of reconciliation in Christ (Ephesians 2:14-16).

3. **Ministry of Peacemaking**:

The church engages in peacemaking and conflict resolution, both within its community and in the world. This peacemaking role is an extension of the reconciliation offered in Christ, as the church seeks to heal divisions and promote peace in all aspects of life (Matthew 5:9).

4. **Discipleship and Sanctification**:

Part of the church's role is to guide believers in the process of sanctification, which involves growing in holiness and Christ-likeness. As believers are sanctified, they more effectively embody and minister reconciliation in their personal and communal lives (Colossians 3:12-14).

5. **Social and Cultural Reconciliation**:

The church also has a role in addressing social and cultural divisions. This involves advocating for justice, mercy, and reconciliation in societal structures, and working towards the healing of divisions caused by factors such as race, ethnicity, and economic disparity (Galatians 3:28).

Theological Foundations

Christ's Reconciliatory Work:

The church's ministry of reconciliation is based on the theological understanding that Christ, through his death and resurrection, reconciled the world to God (Colossians 1:19-22). This reconciliation is not just a spiritual concept but has practical implications for how Christians interact with God, each other, and the world.

The Holy Spirit's Empowerment:

The Holy Spirit empowers the church for this ministry. The Spirit works in believers to produce reconciliation, guiding them in truth, convicting them of sin, and enabling them to live in peace with God and each other (John 16:7-13; Galatians 5:22-23).

Scriptural Mandate:

The church's role in reconciliation is grounded in scriptural mandates such as the Great Commission (Matthew 28:19-20) and the call to be ambassadors for Christ (2 Corinthians 5:20).

Practical Aspects

Evangelism and Missions:

The church is involved in evangelism and missions, spreading the message of reconciliation to new geographical and cultural contexts. This outreach is integral to the church's understanding of its role in God's redemptive plan (Acts 1:8).

Community Engagement:

Local churches engage with their communities in various ways, from social work and community development to interfaith dialogues and peace initiatives. These activities are seen as expressions of the reconciliatory heart of the Gospel.

Pastoral Care:

Pastoral care and counseling are important aspects of the ministry of reconciliation. The church provides support and guidance to individuals and families, helping them to overcome personal conflicts and to live in reconciliation with God and others.

Challenges and Responsibilities

Maintaining Doctrinal Integrity:

While engaging in the ministry of reconciliation, the church must maintain doctrinal integrity, ensuring that its practices and teachings are aligned with biblical truth.

Navigating Cultural and Social Complexities:

The church faces the challenge of navigating cultural and social complexities in its reconciliatory work, striving to be relevant and sensitive to different contexts while remaining faithful to the Gospel.

Promoting Unity in Diversity:

The church must work towards unity within its own body, celebrating diversity while maintaining the unity of the Spirit in the bond of peace (Ephesians 4:3).

The ministry of reconciliation is a comprehensive and dynamic aspect of the church's mission. Rooted in the reconciliatory work of Christ, empowered by the Holy Spirit, and grounded in Scripture, the church is called to be an agent of reconciliation in a fractured world. This ministry encompasses the proclamation of the Gospel, living as a reconciled community, engaging in peacemaking, and advocating for social and cultural reconciliation. The church's effectiveness in this ministry is crucial for demonstrating the power of the Gospel to transform lives and societies.

Living as Reconciled People: Ethics and Lifestyle

In the Christian faith, the concept of living as reconciled people extends beyond the initial act of being reconciled to God through Christ. It encompasses an entire ethical and lifestyle paradigm, rooted in the transformative power of Jesus' sacrifice. This chapter explores how the doctrine of reconciliation influences the moral and practical aspects of a believer's life.

The Ethical Imperative of Reconciliation

1. Moral Transformation:

Reconciliation with God through Christ leads to a moral transformation. This change is not merely behavioral but originates from a renewed heart and mind (Romans 12:1-2). The believer, having been reconciled to God, is called to live in a manner worthy of this reconciliation, exhibiting godly characteristics such as love, kindness, and humility (Colossians 3:12-14).

2. Forgiveness and Peacemaking:

As recipients of God's forgiveness, reconciled individuals are expected to extend forgiveness to others (Ephesians 4:32). This entails a commitment to resolving personal conflicts, promoting peace, and seeking reconciliation in human relationships (Matthew 5:9; 18:21-22).

3. Holiness and Purity:

The ethical life of a reconciled person involves a pursuit of holiness. This pursuit is grounded in the understanding that believers are set apart for God's purposes and called to live in a way that reflects His character (1 Peter 1:15-16).

The Lifestyle of Reconciled People

1. Worship and Devotion:

Reconciled living includes regular worship and devotion. This involves both corporate worship with the church body and personal practices such as prayer, Bible study, and meditation, fostering a deeper relationship with God (Hebrews 10:24-25; Psalm 1:2).

2. Community and Fellowship:

The lifestyle of a reconciled individual is not lived in isolation but within the context of Christian community. Believers are encouraged to engage in fellowship, bear one another's burdens, and build each other up in faith (Galatians 6:2; Hebrews 10:24-25).

3. **Service and Ministry**:

Living as reconciled people includes serving others and participating in various forms of ministry. This service is seen as an outworking of one's faith and a reflection of Christ's love (James 2:17; 1 Peter 4:10).

4. **Witness and Evangelism**:

Reconciled believers are called to be witnesses of the gospel. This involves sharing the message of reconciliation with others, both through words and through living a life that testifies to the transformative power of the gospel (Matthew 28:19-20; 2 Corinthians 5:20).

Ethical Challenges and Considerations

1. **Cultural Engagement**:

Reconciled Christians must navigate the challenges of engaging with a culture that often holds values contrary to biblical teachings. This requires wisdom and discernment, balancing the call to be in the world but not of it (John 17:15-16; 1 Corinthians 9:22).

2. **Ethical Decision-Making**:

Believers are faced with complex ethical decisions in their personal and professional lives. These decisions should be guided by biblical principles, prayer, and the counsel of wise and mature Christians (Proverbs 11:14; Philippians 4:6).

3. **Moral Accountability**:

Living as a reconciled person involves accountability to God and to the Christian community. This accountability helps in maintaining a lifestyle that is consistent with Christian ethics and in receiving support and correction when needed (Galatians 6:1; Hebrews 13:17).

Living as reconciled people under the Christian doctrine is not limited to a spiritual status but is a comprehensive way of life that affects every aspect of a person's existence. It involves a continuous process of transformation, ethical living, community engagement, and service. This lifestyle is a response to the profound work of reconciliation accomplished through Christ and is marked by love, holiness, service, and witness. The reconciled life is not merely about following a set of rules but is a dynamic and growing relationship with God, expressed through ethical behavior, personal integrity, and a commitment to living out the gospel in every area of life.

Edward D. Andrews

CHAPTER 9: Sanctification: The Path of Holiness

The Concept of Sanctification in Scripture

Sanctification is a pivotal concept in Christian theology, particularly in understanding the transformative journey of a believer's life. It represents the process of being made holy, set apart, and consecrated for God's purpose. This chapter delves into the multifaceted aspects of sanctification as presented in Scripture, examining its meaning, process, and implications for a believer's life.

Definition and Scope of Sanctification

1. Holiness and Separation:

Sanctification fundamentally involves being set apart for God's use. It denotes a state of holiness, not in the sense of sinless perfection, but as being distinct from the world and dedicated to God's purposes (1 Peter 2:9). This involves a transformation that affects a believer's heart, mind, and actions.

2. **A Divine Initiative**:

Sanctification is initiated by God. It is He who calls individuals and sets them apart. This is seen in the sanctification of figures like the Levites in the Old Testament and the calling of believers in the New Testament (Numbers 3:12-13; 2 Thessalonians 2:13).

3. **A Process and a Position**:

While sanctification is a positional reality for believers - they are set apart at the moment of salvation - it is also a progressive process. Believers grow in holiness as they live in obedience to God and are continually being transformed into the likeness of Christ (2 Corinthians 3:18).

The Process of Sanctification

1. **Regeneration and Renewal**:

Sanctification begins with regeneration, where a person is born again and receives a new nature in Christ (John 3:3-8). This regeneration leads to a renewed mind and transformed behavior (Romans 12:2).

2. **The Role of the Holy Spirit**:

The Holy Spirit plays a critical role in sanctification. He indwells believers, guiding and empowering them for godly living. The Spirit produces fruit in the life of a believer that reflects Christ's character (Galatians 5:22-23).

3. **Ongoing Transformation**:

Sanctification is an ongoing process. It involves daily dying to sin and living for Christ, continually being purified and molded into Christ's image (Luke 9:23; Philippians 2:12-13).

Sanctification in Various Aspects of Life

1. **Personal Holiness**:

Sanctification impacts personal holiness. Believers are called to live lives that are morally and spiritually pure, resisting sin and pursuing righteousness (1 Peter 1:15-16).

2. **Relational Dynamics**:

Sanctification also affects relationships. Believers are to exhibit love, forgiveness, and grace in their interactions, mirroring the character of Christ (Ephesians 4:32).

3. **Service and Ministry**:

Sanctified individuals are equipped for service. They are given spiritual gifts for the edification of the church and the advancement of God's kingdom (Ephesians 4:11-12).

Challenges in the Sanctification Process

1. **The Struggle with Sin**:

Even though sanctified, believers still face the ongoing struggle with sin due to their fallen nature. This requires constant vigilance and reliance on God's strength (Romans 7:15-25).

2. **Worldly Influences**:

The world's values and practices often conflict with the path of sanctification. Believers must guard against conforming to worldly patterns and instead pursue God's standards (1 John 2:15-17).

3. **Spiritual Disciplines**:

Maintaining spiritual disciplines like prayer, Scripture study, and fellowship is crucial in the sanctification process. These practices nurture spiritual growth and fortify against temptation (Psalm 119:11; Hebrews 10:24-25).

Sanctification is a comprehensive and dynamic aspect of the Christian faith, reflecting both a status and a process. Initiated by God, it involves a believer's whole being and influences every area of life. Through the work of the Holy Spirit, believers are progressively transformed into Christ's likeness, growing in personal holiness, impacting their relationships, and effectively serving in God's kingdom. The journey of sanctification, while challenging due to the ongoing struggle against sin and worldly influences, is integral to the Christian's spiritual maturity and fulfillment of their divine calling.

Old Testament Perspectives on Holiness

In the Old Testament, the concept of holiness is integral and multifaceted, underpinning the relationship between Jehovah God and His people. Holiness, in this context, is not merely moral purity but encompasses a state of being set apart for God's specific purposes. This chapter will explore the dimensions of holiness as presented in the Old Testament, focusing on its implications for individuals, objects, places, and times.

Definition and Nature of Holiness

1. Holiness as Separation for God's Use:

The Hebrew term for "holy," derived from **qa·dhash'**, implies separation or setting apart. In the Old Testament, holiness is primarily about being consecrated for God's purposes (Exodus 19:10-11).

This separation involves a distinct lifestyle, obedience to God's laws, and a rejection of pagan practices (Leviticus 11:44).

2. Holiness of God:

Jehovah God is described as holy, signifying His absolute moral purity, separateness from sin, and distinctness as the sovereign Creator (Isaiah 6:3).

God's holiness is the standard for His people's moral and spiritual conduct (Leviticus 19:2).

3. Holiness in Relation to Sin and Uncleanness:

- Holiness stands in opposition to sin and uncleanness. The Law provided various rituals for purification, symbolizing the removal of impurity and restoration to a state of holiness (Leviticus 16).

Holiness in Personal and Communal Life

1. Individual Holiness:

The Old Testament emphasizes the personal aspect of holiness. Laws about diet, sexual conduct, and personal behavior were meant to cultivate a holy lifestyle (Deuteronomy 14:2-21).

Prophets like Isaiah and Jeremiah called individuals to genuine holiness, not just external ritual compliance (Isaiah 1:16-17).

2. Communal Holiness:

Israel as a nation was set apart as holy. This communal holiness was expressed through obedience to the Mosaic Law and participation in religious festivals (Exodus 19:5-6).

The community's holiness was also maintained through the tabernacle/temple services and the priesthood, which mediated between God and the people (Exodus 28:1-3).

Holiness of Objects and Places

1. Sanctification of Objects:

Objects used in worship, such as the Ark of the Covenant, the Tabernacle, and its furnishings, were sanctified, meaning they were set apart exclusively for worship purposes (Exodus 30:25-29).

These objects were treated with great reverence, symbolizing God's holy presence.

2. Sacred Spaces:

Specific locations were considered holy due to God's presence or activity. Examples include Mount Sinai, the Tabernacle, and the Temple in Jerusalem (Exodus 3:1-5; 19:23).

Jerusalem held a special status as a holy city, being the location of the Temple and the center of Israel's worship (Psalm 48:1-2).

Holiness in Time

1. **Sabbath and Festivals**:

The Sabbath was a holy day, a weekly reminder of God's creation and Israel's deliverance from Egypt (Genesis 2:2-3; Deuteronomy 5:12-15).

Festivals like Passover and the Day of Atonement were holy convocations, times set apart to remember and celebrate God's actions in history (Leviticus 23).

2. **Jubilee Year**:

The Jubilee year was a special time of restoration and liberation, emphasizing social justice and economic reset in alignment with God's holiness (Leviticus 25:10).

In the Old Testament, holiness is a comprehensive concept encompassing individual and communal life, worship practices, and time observance. It is characterized by separation unto God, adherence to His commandments, and a lifestyle reflecting His character. Through the various laws, rituals, and prophetic teachings, the Old Testament lays a foundation for understanding holiness not just as ritual purity but as a dynamic relationship with Jehovah God, marked by obedience, reverence, and a distinct way of life.

Sanctification through Christ: A New Testament View

The concept of sanctification in the New Testament is intricately connected with the person and work of Jesus Christ. This theme represents a significant shift from the Old Testament's focus on external acts and rituals to an emphasis on internal transformation and a personal relationship with God through Christ. This chapter delves into the New Testament understanding of sanctification, as seen through the life, death, resurrection, and teachings of Jesus Christ, and the apostolic doctrine.

The Foundation of Sanctification in Christ

1. Jesus Christ's Role in Sanctification:

Christ's life and sacrificial death are central to the New Testament's understanding of sanctification. By offering Himself as a sinless sacrifice, Christ enables believers to be sanctified — set apart and made holy (Hebrews 9:13-14).

The sanctification offered through Christ is more than ceremonial cleanliness; it involves a deep moral and spiritual renewal (2 Corinthians 5:17).

2. The Blood of Christ:

Unlike the blood of goats and bulls in the Old Testament, the blood of Christ has the power to cleanse believers' consciences from dead works to serve the living God (Hebrews 9:14).

This cleansing is fundamental to sanctification, as it restores the believer's relationship with God, marred by sin.

Sanctification as a Process and a Position

1. Initial Sanctification at Conversion:

When a person puts faith in Christ, they are initially sanctified — set apart as God's possession (Acts 26:18). This act is often referred to as "positional sanctification."

This initial sanctification is an act of God's grace, marking the believer as belonging to Him (Ephesians 1:13-14).

2. Progressive Sanctification in the Christian Life:

Sanctification is also a lifelong process whereby believers grow in holiness (2 Corinthians 3:18). This process is known as "progressive sanctification."

It involves daily being conformed to the image of Christ, a journey that requires the believer's active participation (Romans 12:1-2; Philippians 2:12-13).

The Role of the Holy Spirit

1. **Agent of Sanctification**:

The Holy Spirit plays a crucial role in sanctification, guiding, and empowering believers to live holy lives (Galatians 5:16-25).

The Spirit's work includes convicting of sin, leading to repentance, and enabling obedience to God's will (John 16:8-11; Romans 8:13-14).

2. **Fruit of the Spirit**:

Sanctification is evidenced by the "fruit of the Spirit" — love, joy, peace, patience, kindness, goodness, faithfulness, gentleness, and self-control (Galatians 5:22-23).

These qualities are marks of a life being transformed by the Spirit, reflecting Christ's character.

The Believer's Response and Responsibility

1. **Pursuit of Holiness**:

Believers are called to actively pursue holiness as part of their sanctification (Hebrews 12:14).

This pursuit involves practical steps such as prayer, reading and meditating on Scripture, fellowship with other believers, and practicing spiritual disciplines.

2. **Ongoing Repentance and Renewal**:

Sanctification involves continual repentance and turning away from sin (1 John 1:9).

Believers are exhorted to renew their minds and resist conforming to the world's patterns, embracing instead godly values and behaviors (Romans 12:2).

The Community Aspect of Sanctification

1. **The Church's Role**:

Sanctification is not just an individual pursuit but occurs within the context of the Christian community (Ephesians 4:11-16).

Fellowship, accountability, and mutual encouragement within the church are vital for growth in holiness.

2. **Corporate Worship and Sacraments**:

Participation in corporate worship and sacraments (like Communion) serve as means of grace, aiding the believer's sanctification journey (1 Corinthians 11:23-26).

The Eschatological Dimension

1. **Ultimate Sanctification**:

The New Testament points to a future, complete sanctification that will occur when Christ returns (1 John 3:2-3).

This ultimate sanctification involves the believer being made perfectly holy, free from the presence and power of sin.

2. Hope and Assurance:

The hope of complete sanctification provides assurance and motivation for believers to persevere in their faith and sanctification process (Philippians 1:6).

Sanctification in the New Testament is a rich and multi-dimensional concept centered on the work of Christ and the indwelling of the Holy Spirit. It begins with an initial setting apart at conversion, involves a lifelong process of being conformed to Christ's image, and culminates in the believer's complete transformation at Christ's return. Sanctification is both a gift of grace and a call to active pursuit of holiness, encompassing individual and communal aspects of the Christian life.

The Process of Sanctification: Spiritual Growth and Maturity

Sanctification, in biblical terms, is the process of being made holy, set apart for God's use, and purified from sin. This transformative journey is integral to Christian living, involving a progressive growth in spiritual maturity and holiness. This chapter explores the dynamics of sanctification, emphasizing its practical aspects and implications for a believer's life.

The Biblical Basis of Sanctification

1. Old Testament Foundations:

The Hebrew term "qa·dhash'" reflects the idea of being set apart for a sacred purpose. Examples include the sanctification of the Israelites at Mount Sinai (Exodus 19:10-11) and various ceremonial practices.

Sanctification in the Old Testament often involved external rituals, symbolizing an inner commitment to God.

2. New Testament Expansion:

The Greek term "ha′gi·os" denotes a deeper, more internalized holiness. It is not just about external separation but an inward transformation (2 Corinthians 5:17; Ephesians 4:23-24).

Jesus Christ's role in sanctification is pivotal, providing a way for purification from sin and empowering believers through the Holy Spirit (Hebrews 9:13-14).

The Role of Jesus Christ and the Holy Spirit

1. Christ's Sacrificial Work:

Jesus' sacrifice on the cross is foundational to sanctification, offering believers cleansing from sin and a renewed relationship with God (Hebrews 10:10).

Christ's role as the mediator of the new covenant is crucial for the believer's ongoing sanctification (1 Timothy 2:5).

2. The Holy Spirit's Empowerment:

The Holy Spirit is the agent of sanctification, guiding believers into truth, convicting of sin, and empowering for holy living (John 16:13; Romans 8:13-14).

The fruit of the Spirit (Galatians 5:22-23) is evidence of the Spirit's sanctifying work in a believer's life.

The Process of Sanctification

1.   Initial Sanctification:

This occurs at the point of salvation when a believer is set apart as God's possession (1 Corinthians 6:11).

It is an act of God's grace, marking the beginning of the sanctification journey.

2.   Progressive Sanctification:

This is a lifelong process of being conformed to the image of Christ (Romans 12:1-2; Philippians 2:12-13).

It involves daily choices and actions aligned with God's will, leading to spiritual growth and maturity.

Practical Aspects of Sanctification

1.   Personal Discipline:

Spiritual disciplines such as prayer, Bible study, fasting, and worship are vital for growth in sanctification.

Regular self-examination and repentance are necessary for maintaining a holy life (1 John 1:9).

2.   Community Involvement:

Sanctification also occurs in community, through fellowship with other believers, accountability, and corporate worship (Hebrews 10:24-25).

The church plays a role in nurturing and encouraging individual sanctification.

Challenges and Encouragements

1.   Struggle Against Sin:

Sanctification involves a continual struggle against sin and temptation (Galatians 5:17).

Believers are called to "put off" their old selves and "put on" Christ-like attitudes and behaviors (Ephesians 4:22-24).

2. **Assurance of God's Faithfulness**:

Despite challenges, believers can be assured of God's continuous work in them (Philippians 1:6).

The promise of eventual glorification provides hope and motivation for perseverance (Romans 8:29-30).

Sanctification in Everyday Life

1. **Ethical Living**:

Sanctification manifests in ethical and moral living, reflecting God's character in everyday decisions and actions.

It involves not just avoidance of evil but active pursuit of good, serving others, and spreading the Gospel (Micah 6:8; Matthew 28:19-20).

2. **Holistic Transformation**:

Sanctification encompasses all aspects of life – personal, social, vocational, and spiritual.

It calls for a balanced life, where spiritual growth is integrated into all areas.

Sanctification is not merely a theological concept but a dynamic, ongoing process of spiritual growth and maturation. It involves a synergistic effort between divine grace and human response, leading to a life that increasingly reflects the holiness and character of Christ. Through this journey, believers are equipped to fulfill their calling as

God's set-apart people, empowered to live out their faith in a world that desperately needs the transformative message of the Gospel.

Practical Aspects of Sanctification in Christian Living

Sanctification, as a transformative process of becoming holy and set apart for Jehovah God, has profound practical implications for Christian living. This extensive exploration delves into how sanctification impacts various aspects of a believer's life, shaping their conduct, relationships, and spiritual journey.

1. Daily Conduct and Lifestyle Choices:

Pursuit of Holiness: Believers are called to live lives that reflect Jehovah's holiness (1 Peter 1:15-16). This involves a conscious effort to avoid sinful behavior and cultivate godly qualities.

Spiritual Disciplines: Regular engagement in prayer, Bible study, and worship is essential. These practices deepen one's understanding of God's will and strengthen the commitment to live according to His standards (Psalm 1:1-2).

2. Moral and Ethical Integrity:

Upholding Biblical Standards: Christians are expected to adhere to the moral and ethical teachings of the Bible, eschewing practices that are condemned by Scripture (Ephesians 5:3-5).

Honesty and Justice: Integrity in all dealings, whether personal or professional, is a hallmark of a sanctified life (Proverbs 11:3).

3. Personal Relationships:

Family Life: Sanctification extends to familial roles. Believers are instructed to cultivate Christ-like love and respect within their family units (Ephesians 5:22-33; 6:1-4).

Marriage: As Paul notes in 1 Corinthians 7:14-17, a believing spouse can have a sanctifying influence on their non-believing partner, demonstrating the power of a godly life.

4. Community and Social Interaction:

Influence on Others: Believers are called to be 'salt and light' in the world, positively influencing others towards godliness (Matthew 5:13-16).

Relationship with the World: While in the world, Christians are not to be of the world. This separation involves not conforming to worldly practices and values that are contrary to God's standards (John 17:14-16).

5. Church Participation and Ministry:

Active Church Life: Regular participation in church activities and fellowship is vital for mutual encouragement and growth (Hebrews 10:24-25).

Service and Ministry: Engaging in various forms of ministry and service, both within and outside the church, is an expression of sanctification (1 Peter 4:10-11).

6. Personal Development and Growth:

Spiritual Maturity: Sanctification is a journey towards spiritual maturity, requiring continual growth in understanding and applying biblical truths (Hebrews 6:1).

Character Development: The development of fruits of the Spirit (Galatians 5:22-23) is indicative of sanctification at work in a believer's life.

7. **Response to Trials and Suffering**:

Endurance and Faith: Facing trials with faith and endurance can be a sanctifying experience, producing spiritual strength and maturity (James 1:2-4).

Trust in God: In difficult times, reliance on Jehovah's wisdom and sovereignty is crucial, demonstrating a sanctified trust in His plan (Proverbs 3:5-6).

8. **Holistic Well-being**:

Physical Stewardship: Taking care of one's body, as God's temple, is part of sanctification. This involves healthy living and avoiding harmful practices (1 Corinthians 6:19-20).

Emotional and Mental Health: Maintaining emotional and mental well-being is also important, as it affects one's ability to live out God's purposes effectively (Philippians 4:6-7).

9. **Witnessing and Evangelism**:

Sharing the Gospel: A sanctified life is marked by a commitment to sharing the Gospel with others, fulfilling the Great Commission (Matthew 28:19-20).

Defending the Faith: Being prepared to defend one's faith respectfully and effectively is part of living a sanctified life (1 Peter 3:15).

10. **Stewardship and Financial Integrity**:

Generosity and Giving: Practicing generosity and faithful giving reflects a sanctified attitude towards material possessions (2 Corinthians 9:6-7).

Ethical Financial Practices: Honesty and integrity in financial matters, including business dealings and payment of taxes, are expected of believers (Romans 13:7).

Sanctification in Christian living is an all-encompassing process, influencing every aspect of a believer's life. It calls for a deliberate and continuous effort to live in a manner that is pleasing to Jehovah, reflecting Christ's character in every action, relationship, and decision. This transformative journey is not just about personal holiness but also about being a light in the world, impacting others through the power of a life transformed by God's truth and love.

CHAPTER 10: Salvation: The Ultimate Gift of Grace

Defining Salvation: Biblical Foundations

Salvation, a term that resonates profoundly within Christian theology, encapsulates the idea of deliverance from the direst circumstances—sin, death, and alienation from God. The Christian understanding of salvation is multifaceted, encompassing various dimensions such as justification, sanctification, and glorification. It is essential, therefore, to approach the doctrine of salvation with a comprehensive and scriptural perspective.

The Nature of Salvation

1. **Salvation as Deliverance**:

At its core, salvation in the Christian faith is about deliverance. This deliverance, as described in the Bible, is multifaceted. It includes rescue from sin's bondage (Romans 6:22), deliverance from the clutches of death (1 Corinthians 15:54-57), and liberation from a world marred by sin and under Satanic influence (1 John 5:19). The portrayal of salvation as deliverance is vividly illustrated in the Exodus narrative, where God's act of saving Israel from Egypt prefigures the ultimate deliverance through Christ (1 Corinthians 10:1-2).

2. **Salvation as Reconciliation**:

Salvation also embodies the concept of reconciliation between humanity and God. Sin, as the Bible elucidates, creates a chasm between humans and God (Isaiah 59:2). Through Christ's sacrificial death, this chasm is bridged, enabling a restored relationship with God (2 Corinthians 5:18-19).

3. **Salvation as Transformation**:

The New Testament frequently speaks of salvation as a transformative process. It involves a moral and spiritual regeneration, where a believer is made a new creation in Christ (2 Corinthians 5:17). This transformation is both an instantaneous legal standing before God (justification) and an ongoing process of becoming more like Christ (sanctification).

The Means of Salvation

1. **By Grace Through Faith**:

Ephesians 2:8-9 clearly states that salvation is by grace through faith. This grace is a gift from God, not earned by human efforts or works. Faith, therefore, is the instrumental means by which one receives this grace. It is a trustful reliance on Christ and His atoning sacrifice for sin.

2. **Role of Repentance and Obedience**:

While salvation is not by works, the New Testament emphasizes the role of repentance and obedience as evidence of genuine faith. True faith invariably produces fruits of obedience (James 2:14-26). This obedience is not a means to earn salvation but a response to God's grace in Christ.

The Scope of Salvation

1. **Individual and Cosmic**:

Salvation in the Christian understanding has both an individual and a cosmic dimension. Individually, it refers to personal deliverance from sin and its consequences. Cosmically, it encompasses the restoration of all creation, as promised in Romans 8:19-22, where creation itself will be liberated from its bondage to decay.

2. **Present and Future**:

Salvation is both a present reality and a future hope. Christians are saved in the present sense (Ephesians 2:8), but they also await the future consummation of their salvation (Romans 8:23-25), which includes the resurrection of the body and eternal life with God.

Misconceptions About Salvation

1. **"Once Saved, Always Saved"**:

The doctrine of perseverance of the saints, often summarized as "once saved, always saved," is not supported by a comprehensive reading of Scripture. Passages like

Hebrews 6:4-6 and 2 Peter 2:20-22 warn of the real possibility of falling away from faith. Salvation is thus seen as a dynamic journey, not a one-time event with guaranteed outcomes regardless of one's life choices.

2. **Predestination and Free Will:**

While the Bible speaks of God's sovereignty and predestination (Ephesians 1:5), it also upholds human responsibility and the call to faith and repentance (Acts 17:30). These themes coexist in Scripture, inviting a humble acknowledgment of mystery rather than a rigid doctrinal system that negates either aspect.

In summary, salvation in Christian theology is a rich and multifaceted concept. It involves deliverance from sin and its consequences, a restored relationship with God, and a transformational journey of faith marked by repentance and obedience. It is a gift of grace received through faith, characterized by both individual and cosmic dimensions, encompassing both present experience and future hope.

As we delve deeper into the doctrine of salvation, it becomes evident that it is indeed the ultimate gift of grace, offered by a loving God who desires to reconcile, redeem, and transform His creation. Understanding salvation in its full biblical context is vital for a holistic Christian faith that appreciates the depth of God's redemptive work through Jesus Christ.

The Old Testament View of Salvation: Promises and Prophecies

The Old Testament lays a foundational understanding of salvation, foreshadowing and anticipating the fuller revelation found in the New Testament. It speaks of salvation not only in terms of immediate physical deliverance but also in the context of a broader spiritual and eschatological deliverance, painting a picture of God's redemptive plan for humanity.

1. **Salvation as Physical Deliverance**:

Exodus Narrative: The most striking portrayal of salvation in the Old Testament is the Exodus event (Exodus 14-15). Israel's deliverance from Egyptian bondage is a physical salvation, serving as a type or shadow of the greater spiritual salvation to come through Christ.

Deliverance of the Judges: The cycle of Israel's sin, oppression, repentance, and deliverance through the judges (Judges 2:16-19) is a recurring theme. Each deliverance points to God's faithfulness in saving His people, despite their unfaithfulness.

2. **Salvation as Spiritual Deliverance**:

Prophetic Promises: The prophets, particularly Isaiah and Jeremiah, speak of a future salvation that encompasses not only physical deliverance but also spiritual renewal (Isaiah 53; Jeremiah 31:31-34). These prophecies often merge the concept of immediate national deliverance with the promise of a future, ultimate salvation.

Psalmic Insights: The Psalms frequently mention salvation in the context of deliverance from sin and its consequences (Psalm 51:12). David's psalms, in particular, often express a deep yearning for spiritual salvation and restoration.

3. **Messiah – The Agent of Salvation**:

Messianic Prophecies: The Old Testament prophecies about the Messiah are central to its view of salvation. Passages like Isaiah 53 and Psalm 22 predict a suffering servant who will bear the sins of many. The Messiah is portrayed as the ultimate deliverer, not just from temporal troubles but from the universal problem of sin.

Typologies of Christ: Figures like Joseph, Moses, and David serve as types of Christ, foreshadowing His role as the deliverer and savior. Their lives and actions offer insights into the nature of the Messiah's work of salvation.

4. **Covenantal Framework for Salvation**:

Abrahamic Covenant: The promise made to Abraham (Genesis 12:1-3) is foundational, where salvation is first described as a blessing to all nations, implying a universal scope of salvation that extends beyond Israel.

Mosaic Covenant: While the Mosaic Law highlighted human sinfulness and the need for atonement (Leviticus 17:11), it also pointed forward to the need for a greater sacrifice for sin, ultimately fulfilled in Christ (Hebrews 10:1-4).

5. **The Role of Faith and Obedience**:

Faith of the Patriarchs: The faith of figures like Abraham (Genesis 15:6) is commended as a model of trust in God's promises. Their faith, while resulting in obedient actions, was primarily a reliance on God's promises for future salvation.

Obedience in the Law: The Law emphasized obedience, yet it also underscored human inability to achieve righteousness through one's efforts (Deuteronomy 9:4-6), pointing to the need for a divine intervention for true salvation.

6. **Eschatological Expectations**:

Day of Jehovah: The prophetic writings often speak of the "Day of Jehovah" (Joel 2:1-11), a time of judgment and salvation. This eschatological expectation included both a warning of judgment and a hope of salvation for those who turn to God.

New Creation: Prophets like Isaiah envision a future where God will create a new heaven and a new earth (Isaiah 65:17), symbolizing the ultimate salvation and restoration of all things.

7. **Human Responsibility and Divine Sovereignty**:

Human Responsibility: The Old Testament narratives and laws emphasize human responsibility in responding to God's offer of salvation. The call to repentance and obedience is clear throughout (Deuteronomy 30:19-20).

Divine Sovereignty: Yet, alongside this, there is a strong theme of God's sovereignty in salvation, portraying Him as the initiator and sustainer of the salvific process (Psalm 3:8; Jonah 2:9).

The Old Testament view of salvation is rich and multi-dimensional, encompassing themes of deliverance, covenant, prophecy, and the anticipation of a Messiah. It sets the stage for the New Testament's fuller revelation of salvation through Jesus Christ, providing a backdrop that enhances and deepens the understanding of God's redemptive work. This salvation, while initiated by divine grace, involves human response in faith and obedience, a journey characterized by both assurance and perseverance.

The Accomplishment of Salvation through Jesus Christ

Salvation, in Christian doctrine, reaches its apex in the person and work of Jesus Christ. The New Testament presents Christ as the fulfillment of the Old Testament promises and prophecies, bringing to completion God's redemptive plan for humanity. This chapter explores how Jesus Christ accomplishes salvation, integrating theological insights with scriptural exegesis.

1. The Incarnation: God Becomes Man

John 1:14: The Word became flesh, signifying the divine entering into human experience. The incarnation is foundational to understanding salvation, as it is through Christ's humanity and divinity that the work of redemption is realized.

Philippians 2:6-8: Christ's kenosis (self-emptying) demonstrates the extent of His humility and obedience, essential aspects of His salvific work.

2. The Atonement: Sacrifice for Sin

Romans 3:25-26: Christ is presented as a propitiation for our sins. His death satisfies the just demands of a holy God, reconciling sinful humanity to Him.

Hebrews 9:22-28: Jesus, as the perfect high priest and sacrifice, fulfills and transcends the Old Testament sacrificial system, offering Himself once for all for the atonement of sin.

3. The Victory: Overcoming Sin and Death

1 Corinthians 15:54-57: Christ's resurrection is pivotal in the doctrine of salvation. It signifies victory over death and the guarantee of our resurrection.

Colossians 2:15: Through His death and resurrection, Christ triumphs over principalities and powers, liberating believers from the bondage of sin and Satan.

4. The Justification: Declared Righteous

Romans 5:1-2: Through faith in Christ, believers are justified—declared righteous before God. This legal standing is based on Christ's righteousness, not our own merits.

Galatians 2:16: Paul emphasizes that justification is by faith in Christ, not by works of the Law, highlighting grace as the basis of our salvation.

5. The Sanctification: Process of Being Made Holy

Ephesians 2:10: Believers are created in Christ Jesus for good works. Sanctification is the process by which we are made holy, conforming to the image of Christ.

Philippians 2:12-13: Sanctification involves human effort in response to God's work in us. It is a synergistic process of cooperating with the Holy Spirit.

6. The Intercession: Christ as Our Advocate

Hebrews 7:25: Christ lives to make intercession for believers, ensuring the efficacy of His atoning work. His role as advocate guarantees the continual application of His saving work.

1 John 2:1-2: Jesus is our advocate before the Father, emphasizing His ongoing role in our salvation, especially in moments of failure and sin.

7. The Consummation: Fulfillment of Salvation

Revelation 21:1-4: The final consummation of salvation is depicted as a new heaven and new earth where

God dwells with His people, eradicating sin, death, and suffering.

1 Corinthians 15:24-28: Christ's ultimate reign involves the subjection of all enemies under His feet, culminating in the deliverance of the kingdom to God the Father.

8. The Assurance and Perseverance: Security in Christ

John 10:28-29: Believers are given assurance of salvation, held securely in Christ's hand. However, this assurance does not negate the necessity of perseverance in faith and obedience.

Hebrews 6:4-6; 10:26-29: These passages warn against apostasy, emphasizing the need for continual faithfulness. Salvation is not an irrevocable ticket but a path of enduring faith.

9. The Call to Faith and Repentance

Acts 20:21: The call to salvation in Christ involves both faith and repentance. This dual response highlights the transformation that salvation entails—turning from sin and turning to God in faith.

Romans 10:9-10: Confessing Jesus as Lord and believing in His resurrection are central to the Christian confession and experience of salvation.

The accomplishment of salvation through Jesus Christ is a multidimensional act that encompasses His life, death, resurrection, and ongoing intercession. It is an act of divine initiative, realized through the incarnation and atonement, and applied to believers through faith. This salvation is not only a historical event but an ongoing, dynamic process involving justification, sanctification, and eventual

Edward D. Andrews

glorification. In Christ, believers find the ultimate expression of God's grace, the assurance of His love, and the promise of eternal life, all while being called to a life of faith, obedience, and perseverance.

Responding to the Call of Salvation: Faith and Repentance

In the Christian doctrine of salvation, two fundamental responses are paramount: faith and repentance. These responses are not merely initial steps in the Christian journey but ongoing attitudes that characterize the believer's life. This chapter delves into the biblical understanding of faith and repentance, exploring their significance, nature, and implications in the context of salvation.

1. The Nature of Faith

Definition and Significance: Faith, in the biblical sense, is a trustful reliance on God and His promises. It involves a confident belief not only in God's existence but in His character and word. Hebrews 11:1 defines faith as "the assurance of things hoped for, the conviction of things not seen."

Faith in Christ's Work: Central to Christian faith is the reliance on Jesus Christ's atoning work for salvation. This faith is not a mere intellectual assent but a trust that leads to a personal relationship with Christ (John 3:16; Romans 10:9-10).

2. The Necessity of Faith for Salvation

Ephesians 2:8-9: This passage emphasizes that salvation is by grace through faith. This faith is not self-generated but is a gift from God, excluding any form of human boasting.

Galatians 3:26: Believers are children of God through faith in Christ Jesus. Faith is the means by which one enters into the family of God and enjoys the benefits of salvation.

3. The Role of Repentance in Salvation

Definition and Importance: Repentance involves a change of mind and heart leading to a turning away from sin and turning towards God. It is an indispensable aspect of the Christian response to God's call (Acts 17:30).

Luke 13:3: Jesus' teaching emphasizes the necessity of repentance for salvation. Without repentance, there is no true salvation.

4. The Relationship Between Faith and Repentance

Two Sides of the Same Coin: Faith and repentance are inseparable in the Christian life. Faith involves turning to Christ, while repentance involves turning away from sin. They occur simultaneously and continually in the believer's life.

Acts 20:21: Paul declared that he testified to both Jews and Greeks of "repentance toward God and faith in our Lord Jesus Christ." This highlights the interconnected nature of faith and repentance.

5. The Fruits of True Faith and Repentance

Evidences of Genuine Faith: Genuine faith manifests in obedience and good works (James 2:14-26). While these works do not save, they are the natural outcome of a living faith.

Fruits of Repentance: True repentance results in a changed life. This change is evidenced in new attitudes, behaviors, and priorities (Matthew 3:8).

6. Perseverance in Faith and Repentance

Hebrews 10:26-27; 6:4-6: These passages warn against the danger of falling away. They emphasize the need for perseverance in faith and repentance as evidence of genuine salvation.

Philippians 2:12-13: Believers are called to work out their salvation with fear and trembling, which involves a continual deepening and maturing of faith and repentance.

7. Challenges to Faith and Repentance

The Struggle with Sin: Christians often struggle with sin, which can hinder their walk of faith and repentance. 1 John 1:9 offers assurance that confession leads to forgiveness and cleansing.

The Role of the Church and Community: The Christian community plays a vital role in encouraging and supporting believers in their journey of faith and repentance (Hebrews 10:24-25).

8. The Assurance of Salvation

John 10:28-29: Believers can have assurance of their salvation, knowing they are secure in Christ's hand. However, this assurance should not lead to complacency but to a deeper commitment to faith and repentance.

2 Peter 1:10-11: Peter urges believers to make their calling and election sure through a diligent growth in faith and godly qualities, indicating that assurance comes from a growing and active faith.

9. Responding to the Call

Responding to the call of salvation through faith and repentance is the beginning and the sustaining force of the Christian life. These twin pillars of the Christian response are not one-time acts but ongoing attitudes that shape and define the believer's journey. True faith and repentance lead to a transformative experience, marked by a continual turning away from sin and a turning towards Christ in trust and obedience. This transformative journey is accompanied by the assurance of salvation, rooted in the unchanging character of God and the finished work of Christ, and evidenced in a life characterized by spiritual growth and godly fruits.

The Assurance and Hope of Salvation in Christian Doctrine

The doctrine of salvation within Christianity is not only about the act of being saved but also about the assurance and hope that accompany this salvation. This assurance is a cornerstone of Christian faith, providing comfort and motivation for believers to live a life in accordance with God's will. In this chapter, we will explore the biblical basis for the assurance and hope of salvation, its implications, and how it shapes Christian living.

1. The Biblical Basis for Assurance

John 10:28-29: Jesus' words offer a profound assurance of salvation, affirming that those who belong to Him will never be snatched out of His hand.

Romans 8:38-39: Paul assures believers that nothing can separate them from the love of God in Christ Jesus, underlining the permanence of God's salvific work.

2. The Role of Faith in Assurance

Ephesians 2:8-9: Salvation is described as a gift received through faith, not by works. This faith is itself a gift from God, ensuring that assurance is not based on human merit but on divine promise.

Hebrews 11: The "faith chapter" provides numerous examples of how faith undergirds assurance, demonstrating trust in God's promises despite not seeing them fulfilled in one's lifetime.

3. **The Interplay of Assurance and Perseverance**

Philippians 2:12-13: While believers are assured of their salvation, they are also called to work out their salvation with fear and trembling. This indicates that assurance does not negate the need for perseverance in faith and obedience.

Hebrews 6:4-6; 10:26-27: These passages warn against apostasy, implying that continual faith and repentance are vital for maintaining assurance.

4. **The Hope of Salvation as Future Reality**

Romans 8:23-25: Paul speaks of salvation as a future hope, something believers eagerly await, particularly the redemption of their bodies and the full realization of their status as God's children.

1 Peter 1:3-5: The hope of salvation is described as an inheritance that is imperishable, kept in heaven for believers.

5. **The Assurance of Salvation and Christian Ethics**

James 2:14-26: The epistle of James emphasizes that faith without works is dead. Genuine assurance leads to ethical living and good works, which are evidence of a living faith.

1 John 3:18-20: Assurance is linked to love in action. Our hearts are reassured before God when we love not just in word but in deed and truth.

6. The Assurance of Salvation in Times of Doubt

Psalm 42: The psalmist expresses deep moments of doubt and despair, yet finds hope in remembering God's faithfulness. This suggests that assurance can coexist with, and indeed be strengthened by, periods of doubt and struggle.

2 Corinthians 12:9-10: Paul's experience of weakness and God's sufficient grace illustrates that assurance often shines brightest amidst trials and weaknesses.

7. Warnings Against Presumption

Matthew 7:21-23: Jesus warns that not everyone who calls Him "Lord" will enter the kingdom of heaven, cautioning against a presumptive assurance devoid of true faith and obedience.

Jude 4-5: The letter of Jude reminds believers of the Israelites who were delivered from Egypt but later destroyed due to unbelief, warning against complacency in salvation.

8. Assurance and the Final Judgment

Revelation 20:11-15: The final judgment is a prominent theme in Revelation, where assurance is portrayed as resting on one's name being written in the Book of Life, a metaphor for those who have truly accepted Christ.

2 Peter 3:13-14: Believers are encouraged to live holy and godly lives in anticipation of the new heaven and new earth, where righteousness dwells.

9. **The Assurance and Hope**

The assurance and hope of salvation are integral aspects of Christian doctrine, providing both comfort and challenge to believers. Assurance is rooted in God's promises and faithfulness, not in human merit or effort. This assurance, however, does not lead to passive complacency but calls for active perseverance in faith and obedience. The Christian life, thus assured of salvation, is marked by a hopeful endurance, a transformative ethic, and a forward-looking anticipation of God's ultimate redemption.

APPENDIX A: Challenging Total Depravity: A Biblical Perspective

Understanding Total Depravity in Calvinist Theology

Total Depravity, a cornerstone of Calvinist theology, is a doctrine that asserts the utter sinfulness and moral corruption of humanity as a result of the Fall. It posits that every aspect of human nature is tainted by sin, rendering individuals incapable of coming to God or choosing good without divine intervention. This doctrine forms the foundation for the Calvinist understanding of salvation, predestination, and the sovereignty of God.

Origins and Basis in Scripture

The doctrine of Total Depravity originates from a particular interpretation of biblical texts, notably those that discuss the nature and consequences of sin. Verses such as Romans 3:10-12, which state that "none is righteous, no, not one; no one understands; no one seeks for God," are often cited in support of this doctrine. Additionally, Ephesians 2:1-3, which describes humans as being "dead in the trespasses and sins," is used to argue that people are spiritually dead and incapable of responding to God without His initiating grace.

Implications for Human Will and Morality

Under Total Depravity, human will is seen as enslaved to sin, and every part of a person's being (mind, will, emotions, and flesh) is affected by sin. This doctrine suggests that humans, left to their own devices, will not and cannot choose God or do good in a way that is pleasing to Him. It paints a picture of humanity in desperate need of redemption, wholly reliant on God's grace for salvation.

Calvinist View of Salvation

In Calvinist theology, Total Depravity necessitates unconditional election and irresistible grace. Since humans are utterly depraved, the argument goes, God must elect individuals for salvation based on His sovereign will, not on any foreseen merit or decision on their part. Furthermore, the grace that brings an individual to salvation is irresistible, meaning that those whom God has chosen will inevitably come to faith.

Critique from a Non-Calvinist Perspective

From a non-Calvinist perspective, particularly the one presented here, Total Depravity is seen as overly pessimistic and not entirely consistent with the full witness of Scripture. While acknowledging human sinfulness, this view emphasizes that humans are still capable of responding to God's grace. Scriptures such as John 1:9, which speaks of Christ as the true Light giving light to every person, and Romans 1:20, which talks about God's invisible qualities being clearly seen, are used to argue for the universal ability to perceive and respond to God.

The Role of Free Will in Salvation

The non-Calvinist view upholds the role of human free will in salvation. It contends that while God's grace is necessary for salvation, humans have the freedom to accept or reject this grace. Passages such as Revelation 3:20, where Jesus says, "Behold, I stand at the door and knock. If anyone hears my voice and opens the door, I will come in," are seen as affirming the human capacity to respond to God's initiative.

The Journey of Salvation

Salvation is viewed as a journey or path, where individuals can fall away from faith and later return through repentance. This perspective is supported by passages like Hebrews 6:4-6 and 2 Peter 2:20-22, which warn against the dangers of falling away after having experienced the knowledge of the truth. The emphasis is on the continuous effort and vigilance required in the life of faith, as seen in 2 Peter 1:10-11 and Philippians 2:12-16.

Edward D. Andrews

The Possibility of Apostasy

In this view, there is a real possibility of apostasy, or turning away from the faith, to the point where repentance becomes impossible due to a hardened heart. This is based on scriptural warnings such as Hebrews 10:26-29 and the concept of an "everlasting sin" in Mark 3:28-29. The idea is that a Christian can reach a point where they are beyond repentance, not because God's grace is insufficient, but because they have irrevocably turned away from it.

In conclusion, while Total Depravity highlights important aspects of human sinfulness and the need for divine grace, the non-Calvinist perspective presented here offers a more hopeful view of human ability to respond to God's grace. It emphasizes the role of human free will in accepting salvation, the ongoing nature of the salvation journey, and the real possibility of apostasy. This view seeks to balance the recognition of human sinfulness with the affirmation of God's grace available to all and the human capacity to respond to that grace in faith and obedience.

Scriptural Counterarguments to Total Inability

In Calvinist theology, Total Depravity suggests that due to the Fall, every aspect of human nature is tainted by sin to the extent that humans are incapable of choosing God or doing good without divine intervention. This doctrine leads to the concept of Total Inability, which posits that humans, in their natural state, are utterly unable to turn towards God or seek salvation due to their sinful nature. As a biblically minded person, my perspective diverges from this Calvinist view, focusing on scriptural evidence that supports the potential for human response to God's grace and the role of human free will in the process of salvation.

Human Ability to Seek and Respond to God

The Bible presents various instances and principles that challenge the notion of Total Inability. These passages suggest that humans, while impacted by sin, still retain the capacity to seek and respond to God's initiative.

1. The Universality of God's Call

Romans 1:20 states that God's invisible qualities and divine nature have been clearly perceived in the things that have been made, so people are without excuse.

Acts 17:26-27 illustrates that God's purpose in determining times and boundaries of nations is that people should seek Him and perhaps feel their way toward Him and find Him.

2. Human Responsibility and Choice

Deuteronomy 30:19-20 records God's appeal to choose life by loving and obeying Him, suggesting the ability to respond to God's call.

Joshua 24:15 where Joshua challenges the Israelites to choose whom they will serve, implies the capacity for choice.

3. Invitations to Seek God

Isaiah 55:6-7 encourages seeking the Lord while He may be found and turning to Him for mercy, indicating the possibility of human initiative.

Revelation 3:20 depicts Jesus standing at the door and knocking, implying that individuals can hear His voice and open the door.

The Role of Human Free Will in Cooperation with Divine Grace

Scripture supports the view that while salvation is initiated by God's grace, it involves human cooperation through free will.

1. Free Will in Accepting Salvation

John 1:12-13 speaks of receiving and believing in Jesus to become children of God, highlighting human participation in the process of salvation.

Acts 16:30-31 demonstrates that belief in the Lord Jesus is essential for salvation, indicating a personal decision to believe.

2. Persistence in Faith and the Possibility of Apostasy

Hebrews 6:4-6 and **10:26-29** warn against the dangers of falling away after having been enlightened, indicating that continuance in faith is a matter of personal perseverance.

2 Peter 2:20-22 describes the dire consequences of knowing the way of righteousness and then turning back, underscoring the responsibility to persist in faith.

3. Active Participation in Salvation

Philippians 2:12-13 advises working out one's salvation with fear and trembling, which involves active engagement with God's work in one's life.

James 2:14-26 emphasizes that faith without works is dead, asserting that genuine faith is demonstrated through actions.

Scriptural Evidence Against the Irreversibility of Salvation

The idea that salvation, once received, cannot be forfeited is challenged by several biblical passages that imply the need for continual faithfulness and the possibility of losing salvation.

1. **Warnings Against Falling Away**

Hebrews 6:4-6 and **10:26-27** warn about the peril of falling away after having received knowledge of the truth, suggesting that salvation can be jeopardized.

2 Peter 1:10-11 advises believers to make their calling and election sure by continuing in righteous deeds, implying the need for ongoing diligence.

2. **The Need for Endurance in Faith**

- **Matthew 24:13** states that those who endure to the end will be saved, indicating that perseverance in faith is crucial for final salvation.

- **Revelation 2:10** encourages faithfulness until death to receive the crown of life, highlighting the importance of enduring faith.

The scriptural evidence presents a more nuanced view of human nature and salvation than that offered by Total Depravity and Total Inability. While acknowledging human sinfulness and the necessity of divine grace for salvation, these passages suggest that humans are capable of seeking God and responding to His call. They emphasize the role of human free will in accepting and cooperating with God's grace, the need for persistent faith, and the real possibility of apostasy. This perspective aligns with the understanding that salvation is a dynamic journey, where continual faithfulness and active participation are essential. It upholds the biblical balance of God's sovereignty in initiating salvation and human responsibility in responding to and persevering in that grace.

The Role of Human Will and Responsibility in Salvation

As a biblically minded person, it's essential to explore the role of human will and responsibility in the doctrine of salvation. This perspective challenges the Calvinist view of Total Depravity, which asserts that humans are utterly incapable of choosing God or doing good without divine intervention. A thorough examination of Scripture reveals a more nuanced understanding, emphasizing human responsibility and the dynamic nature of salvation.

1. Human Free Will and the Call to Choose God

The Bible consistently presents the concept of choice, indicating that humans have the free will to respond to God's call.

Deuteronomy 30:19-20: God sets before the people life and death, blessings and curses, urging them to choose life by loving and obeying Him.

Joshua 24:15: Joshua challenges the Israelites to choose whom they will serve, emphasizing the ability and responsibility to make a choice.

2. The Human Response to Divine Initiative

Scripture illustrates that while God initiates salvation, human response plays a crucial role.

John 1:12-13: The Gospel of John speaks of receiving Christ and believing in His name as prerequisites to becoming children of God, highlighting a human action in response to divine initiative.

Acts 16:30-31: The Philippian jailer's question about salvation and Paul's response underscore the necessity of human belief in the process of salvation.

3. The Call to Repentance and Faith

The New Testament especially emphasizes repentance and faith as key aspects of salvation, both of which involve human will.

Mark 1:15: Jesus begins His ministry proclaiming the need for repentance and belief in the gospel.

Acts 20:21: Paul testifies to both Jews and Greeks of repentance toward God and faith in our Lord Jesus Christ.

4. The Need for Ongoing Faith and Perseverance

The doctrine of perseverance highlights the continuous nature of faith and the need for ongoing commitment.

Colossians 1:22-23: Paul speaks of being presented holy and blameless if one continues in the faith, stable and steadfast.

Hebrews 10:36: The writer of Hebrews emphasizes the need for perseverance to receive what is promised.

5. The Warning Against Apostasy

Edward D. Andrews

Several passages warn against the danger of falling away, which implies the possibility of such an event.

Hebrews 6:4-6: This passage warns against the impossibility of restoring those who have fallen away, indicating that such a falling away is a real possibility.

2 Peter 2:20-22: Peter describes the dire state of those who have known the way of righteousness and then turned back.

6. The Relationship Between Faith and Works

The epistle of James brings to light the relationship between faith and works, stressing that faith without works is dead.

James 2:14-26: James argues that faith, if it does not have works, is dead, suggesting that genuine faith manifests in actions.

7. The Dynamic Nature of Salvation

Salvation is portrayed as a dynamic process, not a one-time event, involving human cooperation with divine grace.

Philippians 2:12-13: Paul encourages believers to work out their salvation with fear and trembling, indicating an ongoing process.

1 Corinthians 9:27: Paul speaks of disciplining his body and keeping it under control, lest after preaching to others, he himself should be disqualified, reflecting the ongoing nature of maintaining one's salvation.

8. The Unforgivable Sin and Eternal Consequences

Scripture speaks of an unforgivable sin, suggesting that there are eternal consequences for certain choices.

Mark 3:28-29: Jesus speaks of the unforgivable sin against the Holy Spirit, indicating that certain choices can lead to irreversible spiritual consequences.

Hebrews 10:26-27: The writer warns of a fearful expectation of judgment for those who deliberately keep on sinning after receiving the knowledge of the truth.

The scriptural evidence challenges the Calvinist view of Total Depravity and Total Inability by emphasizing human will and responsibility in the process of salvation. The Bible portrays humans as capable of responding to God's grace, requiring ongoing faith and perseverance, and warns of the real danger of apostasy. Salvation is not a static state achieved once and for all but a dynamic journey that involves continuous faith, repentance, and obedience. This understanding upholds the sovereignty of God in salvation while affirming human responsibility, maintaining a balanced and biblically grounded view of the doctrine of salvation.

Illustrations of Free Will and Divine Grace in Scripture

The interplay between free will and divine grace is a fundamental aspect of Christian theology, particularly in the context of salvation. This perspective, divergent from Calvinist theology, recognizes human agency in the salvation process while affirming the indispensable role of divine grace. The Scriptures offer numerous illustrations that elucidate this relationship.

1. The Call to Choose Life – Deuteronomy 30:19-20

Moses presents the Israelites with a choice between life and death, blessings and curses. The invitation to choose life is an appeal to human free will, urging them to love and obey God. This passage indicates that while God provides the path to salvation, the choice to walk in it rests with the individual.

2. The Parable of the Sower – Matthew 13:3-23

Jesus' parable illustrates various responses to the word of God. The different types of soil represent different human responses to divine revelation. This parable suggests that while the message of salvation (the seed) is a divine initiative, the reception and fruitfulness depend on the condition of the heart (the soil), which is a matter of human free will.

3. The Call of Zacchaeus – Luke 19:1-10

Zacchaeus' story exemplifies the synergy of divine grace and human response. Jesus initiates the interaction, but Zacchaeus responds with eagerness and repentance, leading to his salvation. This narrative highlights the responsiveness of the human heart to God's grace.

4. The Prodigal Son – Luke 15:11-32

This parable is a powerful depiction of free will and grace. The younger son's decision to return home is a metaphor for repentance, an exercise of free will. The father's compassionate response symbolizes divine grace, welcoming and restoring the son without merit.

5. Peter's Denial and Restoration – John 18:15-27; 21:15-19

Peter's denial of Christ and subsequent restoration illustrate the dynamics of human frailty and divine grace. Despite Peter's failure, Christ graciously restores him, highlighting the coexistence of human weakness with the redemptive power of grace.

6. Paul's Conversion – Acts 9:1-19

Paul's conversion is a striking example of divine grace interrupting a human life. While Paul's transformation is initiated by Christ's direct intervention, Paul's subsequent response and missionary work reflect his exercise of free will in service to the Gospel.

7. The Message to the Churches in Revelation

The messages to the seven churches in Revelation (Revelation 2-3) combine warnings, commendations, and calls to repentance. These messages respect the autonomy of each church while underscoring the necessity of divine grace for spiritual vitality and endurance.

8. The Exhortation to Work Out Salvation – Philippians 2:12-13

Paul's exhortation to the Philippians to work out their salvation "with fear and trembling" respects human agency while acknowledging that it is God who works in them to will and to act. This interplay exemplifies the cooperative nature of salvation involving both divine enablement and human effort.

9. The Invitation in Revelation 22:17

The closing chapters of Revelation extend an open invitation: "Let the one who is thirsty come; let the one who desires take the water of life without price." This invitation respects human volition, offering grace freely while allowing for the individual's response.

10. Faith and Works – James 2:14-26

James emphasizes that faith, if not accompanied by action, is dead. This perspective recognizes that while salvation is initiated by grace through faith, it is authenticated and completed by works that evidence genuine faith.

The scriptural illustrations mentioned above demonstrate that while salvation is fundamentally a work of divine grace, human free will plays a crucial role in responding to God's grace. These passages collectively reject the notion of total inability as posited in Calvinist theology and affirm the cooperative nature of salvation. They highlight the Biblical balance between God's sovereignty and human responsibility, emphasizing that the journey of faith involves both divine initiative and human response.

Reconciling God's Sovereignty with Human Choice

The reconciliation of God's sovereignty with human choice is a profound and intricate subject in Christian theology. This exploration challenges the Calvinist doctrine of Total Depravity, which posits that human beings are entirely incapable of choosing God or doing good without divine intervention due to their inherent sinfulness. The scriptures, however, present a more nuanced picture that acknowledges God's supreme authority while simultaneously affirming human responsibility and the capacity for choice.

1. The Sovereignty of God in Salvation

The Bible unequivocally declares God's sovereignty in all things, including the realm of salvation.

Ephesians 1:4-5: God's predestining of believers to adoption through Jesus Christ is an expression of His sovereign will.

Romans 9:15-16: Paul emphasizes that God's mercy is not contingent on human will or effort, but on God's mercy alone.

2. The Agency of Human Choice

Scripture also consistently presents the concept of human choice and responsibility in the context of salvation.

Deuteronomy 30:19-20: God sets before the Israelites life and death, blessing and curse, urging them to choose life by loving and obeying Him.

Joshua 24:15: Joshua challenges the Israelites to choose whom they will serve, emphasizing the human responsibility to make a choice.

3. The Paradox of Divine Sovereignty and Human Responsibility

The biblical narrative often presents scenarios where divine sovereignty and human choice intersect in ways that are difficult to fully comprehend but are not contradictory.

Genesis 50:20: Joseph acknowledges that what his brothers intended for evil, God intended for good, illustrating the convergence of human actions and divine purpose.

Acts 2:23: Peter declares that Jesus was handed over by God's set purpose and foreknowledge, and yet the people were responsible for His crucifixion.

4. The Call to Repentance and Faith

Throughout the New Testament, there is a recurrent call to repentance and faith, both of which presuppose the ability to respond.

Mark 1:15: Jesus begins His ministry proclaiming the need for repentance and belief in the gospel.

Acts 17:30: Paul asserts that God commands all people everywhere to repent.

5. Faith as a Response to Divine Initiative

The concept of faith in Scripture is often presented as a response to God's initiative, a synergy of divine grace and human response.

John 6:44: Jesus states that no one can come to Him unless the Father draws them, indicating God's initiative, yet this drawing requires a response of faith.

Ephesians 2:8-9: Salvation is described as a gift from God, received through faith, which is itself a response to God's grace.

6. The Dynamics of Perseverance and Apostasy

The New Testament contains warnings about apostasy, implying the need for perseverance in faith, which involves a continued choice to follow Christ.

Hebrews 6:4-6

Calvinism's Total Depravity doctrine posits that every aspect of humanity is tainted by sin, thus rendering individuals incapable of coming to God without divine intervention. This viewpoint is often linked to a belief in predestination, where God elects certain individuals for salvation.

Hebrews 6:4-6 (UASV):

4 For in the case of those who have once been enlightened and have tasted of the heavenly gift and have been made partakers of the Holy Spirit, 5 and have tasted the good word of God and the powers of the age to come, 6 and then have fallen away, it is impossible to renew them again

to repentance, since they again crucify to themselves the Son of God and put him to public shame.

Exegetical Analysis:

1. **Contextual Understanding**: This passage is addressing believers, not the unregenerate. The description of those who have been "enlightened" and have "tasted of the heavenly gift" indicates a genuine experience with divine truths, not a superficial encounter.

2. **Human Agency**: The passage implies human agency in the decision to "fall away." If humans were totally depraved in the Calvinistic sense, their initial turning towards God (enlightenment and tasting the heavenly gift) would be inexplicable without divine election, and their subsequent apostasy would be impossible if God's electing grace is irrevocable.

3. **Falling Away**: The possibility of "falling away" after having shared in the Holy Spirit challenges the notion of Total Depravity. If individuals are so depraved that they cannot seek God without irresistible grace, then their falling away suggests a resistance to or rejection of that grace, contradicting the Calvinistic understanding of irresistible grace (a component of Total Depravity).

4. **Responsibility and Repentance**: The warning against falling away and the difficulty of restoring such a person to repentance imply personal responsibility. Total Depravity, as understood in Calvinism, diminishes this personal responsibility by ascribing all initiatives of faith and repentance to God's unaided action.

5. **Theological Implications**: The passage, therefore, presents a challenge to the Calvinistic interpretation of Total Depravity. It suggests that individuals, even after experiencing God's grace, retain the capacity to turn away, implying a degree of free will inconsistent with Total Depravity.

Hebrews 6:4-6, when understood within its context and with a focus on the human agency and responsibility it implies, presents a significant challenge to the Calvinistic doctrine of Total Depravity. It suggests a more cooperative dynamic between divine grace and human response in the process of salvation.

Hebrews 10:26-29

26 For if we go on sinning deliberately after receiving the accurate knowledge[1] of the truth, there no longer remains a sacrifice for sins, 27 but a fearful expectation of judgment, and a fury of fire that will consume the adversaries. 28 Anyone who has set aside the Law of Moses dies without mercy on the evidence of two or three

---

[1] **Accurate Knowledge**: (ἐπίγνωσις epignōsis) This is a strengthened or intensified form of *gnosis* (*epi*, meaning "additional"), meaning "true," "real," "full," "complete" or "accurate," depending upon the context. It is a personal recognition where one understands something clearly and distinctly or as true and valid. Paul and Peter alone use *epignosis*. Paul uses the term 15 times, while Peter uses it four times. Paul wrote about some who were "always learning and yet never able to come to accurate knowledge of truth." (2 Ti 3:6–7) He also prayed for those in the Colossian church, who clearly had some knowledge of the will and purposes of the Father, for they had become Christians, "that [they] may be filled with the accurate knowledge of his will in all spiritual wisdom and understanding." (Col 1:9) All Christians should desire to obtain or achieve accurate knowledge of God's Word. (Eph 1:15–17; Php 1:9; 1 Ti 2:3–4), It is crucial in one's effort at putting on the new person that Paul spoke of, and in gaining peace.—Rom. 1:28; Eph. 1:17; Phil. 1:9; Col. 1:9–10; 3:10; 1 Tim 2:4; 2 Pe 1:2.

witnesses. [29] How much worse punishment, do you think, will be deserved by the one who has trampled underfoot the Son of God, and has profaned the blood of the covenant by which he was sanctified, and has outraged the Spirit of grace?

Exegetical Analysis:

1. **Intentional Sin After Enlightenment**: The passage warns against deliberate sinning after receiving the truth. This implies a conscious and voluntary rejection of the truth, which is inconsistent with the Calvinistic view that the unregenerate are utterly unable to respond positively to God's truth without regeneration.

2. **Human Responsibility**: The passage emphasizes human responsibility. The warning about judgment presupposes that the readers, having understood the truth, have the ability to choose their actions. In Total Depravity, the capacity for such a choice would be absent without divine intervention.

3. **Sanctification and Apostasy**: It speaks of someone who was "sanctified" yet still could choose to reject (trample underfoot) the Son of God. This challenges the notion of Total Depravity where sanctification would be a result of irresistible grace, implying that such a falling away shouldn't be possible if God has sovereignly elected an individual.

4. **Severity of Punishment**: The passage compares the severity of punishment under the law of Moses with that for those who reject Christ. This comparison assumes that the listeners, aware of the truth, have the capacity to understand and respond to such a warning, which suggests a level of moral

and spiritual awareness incompatible with Total Depravity.

5. **Spirit of Grace**: The mention of "outraging the Spirit of grace" indicates that it's possible to resist or reject the influence of the Holy Spirit. This resistance is at odds with the Calvinistic view that the grace of God in the regeneration of the elect is irresistible.

Hebrews 10:26-29, with its focus on the conscious, deliberate actions of those who have received and understood the truth, presents a significant challenge to the Calvinistic doctrine of Total Depravity. It suggests that humans, even after receiving the knowledge of the truth, have the capacity to make genuine choices regarding their faith and actions, implying a degree of free will and moral responsibility that Total Depravity does not accommodate.

2 Peter 2:20-22: Peter describes the dire state of those who have known the way of righteousness and then turned back.

7. The Role of Works in Demonstrating Faith

The epistle of James highlights that genuine faith is demonstrated through works, a theme that underscores the interactive nature of faith and works in the life of a believer.

- **James 2:14-26**: James argues that faith, if it does not have works, is dead, suggesting that true faith results in actions that align with God's will.

8. The Final Judgment and Human Accountability

The Bible's teaching on the final judgment underscores human accountability for choices made in life.

- **Matthew 25:31-46**: The parable of the sheep and the goats illustrates that individuals will be judged based on their actions, reflecting the importance of human choices in response to God's grace.

In conclusion, the scriptural witness presents a complex yet coherent picture of God's sovereignty and human choice in the realm of salvation. This perspective recognizes the depth of human sinfulness but does not negate the human capacity to respond to God's grace. It holds in tension the biblical truths of God's sovereign will in electing and saving sinners, and the genuine responsibility of humans to repent, believe, and persevere in faith. This balance is essential for a comprehensive understanding of the doctrine of salvation, affirming the richness of divine grace and the significant role of human response in the journey of faith.

Edward D. Andrews

APPENDIX B: Unraveling Unconditional Election: A Scriptural Examination

The Concept of Unconditional Election in Calvinism

Unconditional election is a key doctrine in Calvinism that pertains to predestination. It describes God's actions and motives prior to the creation of the world, when He predestined some people, known as the elect, to receive salvation, while others were left to continue in their sins and receive the just punishment, eternal damnation, for their transgressions of God's law as outlined in the Old and New Testaments of the Bible.

This doctrine asserts that God's choices were made according to His own purposes, independent of any conditions or qualities related to those individuals. This means that God's election does not foresee an action or condition on our part that induces Him to save us. Instead, it rests on God's sovereign decision to save whomever He is pleased to save.

Unconditional election does not mean that there will be people in heaven who do not want to be there, nor will there be people in hell who wanted to be saved but could not be because they were not elect **3**. It also does not imply that there is no cause for the electing grace of God. Rather, it simply means that there is no cause or condition in us.

The doctrine of unconditional election was first articulated and popularized by the 4th century Church Father Augustine of Hippo during his debates with Pelagius **1**. It represents the second letter of the acronym TULIP, which is commonly used to enumerate the five points of Calvinism, also known as the Doctrines of Grace.

Unconditional election is considered a fundamental truth in the Reformed faith and is seen as the very heart and core of the gospel. It is the basis of all the comfort and assurance of the people of God in the midst of the world.

Biblical Instances of Conditional Divine Favor

The doctrine of unconditional election, a cornerstone of Calvinist theology, posits that God's selection of certain individuals for salvation is based solely on His will and not on any foreseen merit or action on the part of those chosen. However, a scriptural examination reveals numerous instances where divine favor appears to be conditional, tied to human response and actions. This perspective, which views salvation as a journey where individuals can stray and return to the path, aligns with the numerous biblical narratives that underscore the role of human agency in receiving divine favor.

The Covenant with Abraham

The covenant God establishes with Abraham in Genesis is foundational in understanding the nature of divine promises and human responsibility. God's promise to Abraham in Genesis 12:1-3 is initiated by divine grace, yet its fulfillment is continually linked with Abraham's faith and obedience, as seen in Genesis 15:6 and 22:18. Abraham's willingness to leave his homeland and later to offer Isaac as a sacrifice are key moments that activate God's promises, suggesting a synergy between divine initiative and human response.

The Mosaic Covenant

The Mosaic Covenant, established in Exodus 19-24, further illustrates the conditional aspect of divine favor. God's promise to make Israel a "kingdom of priests and a holy nation" is contingent upon their obedience to His commandments, as seen in Exodus 19:5-6. The blessings and curses outlined in Deuteronomy 28 further underscore this conditional relationship, linking Israel's prosperity in the land to their adherence to the law.

Davidic Covenant

The covenant with David, as recorded in 2 Samuel 7, includes an unconditional promise of a perpetual dynasty, yet the fulfillment of this promise is seen in the context of the kings' faithfulness. The subsequent history of Judah demonstrates that the security and prosperity of David's descendants are linked with their obedience to God, as highlighted in 1 Kings 9:4-5.

Prophetic Calls for Repentance

The prophetic literature is replete with instances where divine favor is contingent upon Israel's repentance and return to God. Prophets like Jeremiah and Ezekiel call the people to repent to avert disaster and receive restoration, indicating a conditional aspect of receiving God's mercy, as seen in Jeremiah 18:7-10 and Ezekiel 33:11.

New Testament Teachings on Faith and Works

In the New Testament, the teachings of Jesus and the apostles often link divine favor with faith and obedience. Jesus' parables, such as the Parable of the Sower in Matthew 13, underscore the importance of a receptive heart to God's word for salvation to take root. The messages to the churches in Revelation 2-3 further illustrate the conditional nature of God's favor, as they include both commendations for faithfulness and warnings against complacency and disobedience.

The Role of Faith in Salvation

Paul's epistles, while emphasizing faith as the basis for salvation, also underscore the necessity of a living faith manifested through love and obedience. Galatians 5:6 speaks of faith working through love, and Romans 2:6-8 indicates that eternal life is for those who by persistence in doing good seek glory, honor, and immortality.

Warnings Against Apostasy

The New Testament contains serious warnings against apostasy, suggesting that the perseverance in faith is crucial for maintaining one's standing in God's favor. Hebrews 6:4-6 and 10:26-31 warn of the grave consequences of turning away after having received the knowledge of the truth, indicating that continued faithfulness is necessary for final salvation.

The Parables of Jesus

Jesus' parables often illustrate the conditional aspects of receiving the kingdom of God. The Parable of the Great Banquet in Luke 14:15-24 invites all to partake, yet the actual participation is based on the guests' willingness to accept the invitation. Similarly, the Parable of the Talents in Matthew 25:14-30 demonstrates that the servants' future is determined by their use of the resources entrusted to them.

The Johannine Emphasis on Abiding

In the Johannine literature, particularly the Gospel of John and the first epistle, the concept of abiding in Christ is crucial for maintaining divine favor. John 15:1-10 speaks of remaining in Jesus as a vine to bear fruit, implying an ongoing, active relationship with Christ as essential for spiritual vitality.

The Message of James on Faith and Works

The Epistle of James provides a compelling argument for the integration of faith and works in the experience of divine favor. James 2:14-26 argues that faith without works is dead, suggesting that a genuine faith necessarily involves actions that reflect a transformed life.

Paul's Teachings on Grace and Election

While Pauline theology is often cited in support of unconditional election, a closer examination of Paul's letters reveals a more nuanced understanding. Romans 11:22, for instance, speaks of the kindness and sternness of God: kindness to those who continue in His kindness, and sternness to those who fall. This suggests a dynamic relationship with God that involves human faithfulness.

The scriptural examination of divine favor reveals a complex interaction between divine grace and human choice. The biblical narrative, from the patriarchs to the New Testament, consistently illustrates that while God's grace initiates and sustains the covenant relationship, human response in faith and obedience plays a significant role in the experience and continuation of that favor. This perspective challenges the notion of unconditional election and underscores the dynamic nature of salvation as a journey involving both divine initiative and human responsibility.

The Universality of God's Call and Human Response

In examining the doctrine of salvation from a biblical perspective, it's crucial to explore the dynamics of God's universal call and the corresponding human response. This exploration challenges the Calvinist doctrine of Unconditional Election, which posits that God predestines certain individuals to salvation without regard to their actions or choices. Scripture, however, presents a broader and more inclusive view of salvation, emphasizing the universal nature of God's call and the vital role of human response in the salvation process.

The Universal Nature of God's Call

The Bible frequently depicts God's invitation to salvation as universal, extended to all humanity without partiality.

1. **John 3:16-17**: "For God so loved the world that he gave his only Son, that whoever believes in him should not perish but have eternal life. For God did not send his Son into the world to condemn the world, but in order that the world might be saved through him." This passage clearly indicates God's desire for the salvation of all humanity, not a preselected few.

2. **1 Timothy 2:3-4**: "This is good, and it is pleasing in the sight of God our Savior, who desires all people to be saved and to come to the knowledge of the truth." Paul's words to Timothy affirm God's desire for all to be saved, suggesting a universal call.

3. **2 Peter 3:9**: "The Lord is not slow to fulfill his promise as some count slowness, but is patient toward you, not wishing that any should perish, but that all should reach repentance." Peter emphasizes God's patience and His wish for all to come to repentance, again underscoring the universality of the divine call.

Human Response to Divine Call

Human response to God's call is a consistent theme in Scripture, highlighting the role of human agency in the salvation process.

1. **Acts 2:38**: "And Peter said to them, 'Repent and be baptized every one of you in the name of Jesus Christ for the forgiveness of your sins, and you will receive the gift of the Holy Spirit.'" Peter's call to repentance was to everyone, suggesting that all have the opportunity and responsibility to respond.

2. **Romans 10:13**: "For 'everyone who calls on the name of the Lord will be saved.'" Paul's quotation from Joel 2:32 emphasizes the universal opportunity for salvation through the act of calling upon the Lord.

3. **Revelation 22:17**: "The Spirit and the Bride say, 'Come.' And let the one who hears say, 'Come.' And let the one who is thirsty come; let the one who desires take the water of life without price." This invitation at the end of the Bible is inclusive, extending the offer of salvation to whoever wishes to take it.

The Role of Faith and Works in Salvation

The New Testament consistently ties salvation to faith, which is a human response to God's grace, and to works, which evidence genuine faith.

1. **James 2:17-26**: James argues that faith without works is dead, suggesting that genuine faith naturally results in actions that align with God's will.

2. **Ephesians 2:8-10**: While Paul emphasizes that salvation is by grace through faith and not by works, he also states that we are created in Christ Jesus for good works.

Parables of Jesus on Human Choice

Jesus' parables often highlight the need for human response to God's invitation.

1. **Parable of the Great Banquet (Luke 14:15-24)**: This parable illustrates that those who respond to the invitation will partake in the kingdom of God, while those who refuse will miss out, underscoring the importance of response.

2. **Parable of the Sower (Matthew 13:3-23)**: The different responses to the seed, the word of God, signify the various ways people respond to God's message.

Prophetic Calls for Repentance

The prophetic books are filled with calls for repentance, indicating that a response to God's call is necessary for restoration and salvation.

1. **Jeremiah 18:7-10**: God's message through Jeremiah shows that a nation's destiny can change based on its response to His words.

2. **Ezekiel 33:11**: God expresses His desire that the wicked turn from their ways and live, again highlighting the universal nature of His call and the required human response.

The scriptural examination reveals a balanced view of salvation, combining the universality of God's call with the necessity of human response. This perspective aligns with the understanding that salvation is not exclusively predetermined by divine election but is offered to all, requiring a response of faith and repentance. It acknowledges both God's sovereign initiative in providing salvation and the human responsibility to respond to His gracious offer. This understanding of salvation as a journey emphasizes the ongoing nature of faith and the possibility of falling away, highlighting the need for perseverance and continual reliance on God's grace.

Examining Predestination and Foreknowledge in Scripture

The concepts of predestination and foreknowledge, especially in the context of salvation, have been central to Christian theological debate. The Calvinist doctrine of Unconditional Election hinges on a specific understanding of these terms, suggesting that God predestines certain individuals to salvation irrespective of their actions or decisions. However, a closer examination of Scripture, particularly in light of the Simple Foreknowledge view, reveals a more complex interaction between divine foreknowledge, human freedom, and God's sovereign plan.

1. Biblical Foundations of Foreknowledge

Foreknowledge in Scripture implies God's omniscience, His ability to know all things, including future events, without this knowledge causally determining those events.

Isaiah 46:9-10: God declares that He makes known the end from the beginning, indicating His foreknowledge of events. However, this does not imply that He predetermines every human action.

1 Peter 1:2: Peter speaks of believers as chosen according to the foreknowledge of God, suggesting that God's knowledge of future events includes human responses to His grace.

2. Predestination in the Context of God's Plan

The Bible does speak of predestination, but this is often in the context of God's overarching plan of salvation rather than individual election.

Ephesians 1:4-5: Paul talks about believers being predestined for adoption. This can be understood as God's plan for the salvation of humanity rather than the predestination of specific individuals.

Romans 8:29-30: These verses, often cited in support of predestination, can be interpreted as God's foreknowledge of those who would freely choose Him, thus predestining them to be conformed to the image of His Son.

3. The Role of Human Free Will

Scripture consistently upholds human free will, allowing for genuine human response to God's offer of salvation.

Deuteronomy 30:19: God sets before the Israelites life and death, urging them to choose life. This indicates the presence of a genuine choice.

Joshua 24:15: Joshua's challenge to choose whom to serve underscores the capacity for human decision in matters of faith.

4. The Parables of Jesus and Human Responsibility

Jesus' parables often highlight the role of human responsibility and choice in relation to God's kingdom.

Parable of the Sower (Matthew 13:3-23): Different responses to the word of God show that human reception of divine truth varies and is contingent on individual choice.

Parable of the Prodigal Son (Luke 15:11-32): The son's return to the father is a decision, depicting repentance and acceptance of the father's grace.

5. Foreknowledge and the Crucifixion

The New Testament presents the crucifixion of Christ as a key event in God's plan known beforehand, yet it involves human actions carried out in freedom.

Acts 2:23: Peter states that Jesus was handed over by God's deliberate plan and foreknowledge, yet He was killed by the hands of lawless men, implying that human actions were freely carried out within God's foreknown plan.

6. Conditional Aspects of Salvation

Scriptural narratives and teachings often present salvation as contingent on faith and obedience, suggesting that human response influences one's relationship with God.

Hebrews 11: The "faith chapter" demonstrates that the ancients were commended for their faith, which involved active response to God's promises.

James 2:14-26: James argues that faith without works is dead, showing that genuine faith necessarily involves corresponding actions.

7. Foreknowledge as a 'Barometer'

The analogy of foreknowledge as a barometer helps in understanding its relationship with free will. Just as a barometer accurately reads the weather but does not cause it, God's foreknowledge of future events does not cause those events. Instead, it is a perfect understanding of what free moral agents will choose to do.

8. Apostasy and Perseverance

Scriptures warning against apostasy and urging perseverance imply that continued faith and obedience are necessary for salvation, countering the idea of predestined, irrevocable salvation.

2 Peter 2:20-22: The possibility of falling away after having known the way of righteousness indicates that perseverance in faith is not guaranteed.

Hebrews 6:4-6: The stern warning against falling away suggests that those who have once embraced the faith can still turn away, contradicting the notion of unconditional perseverance.

The concept of Simple Foreknowledge posits that God possesses complete knowledge, encompassing even future events that are contingent. However, this knowledge does not dictate or determine these events. Advocates of Simple Foreknowledge maintain that human freedom and God's foreknowledge can coexist harmoniously, as God's foreknowledge does not causally influence human decisions.

To put it simply, an event does not transpire because God has foreknowledge of it. Instead, God has foreknowledge of the event because it is destined to occur. The event is logically prior to the foreknowledge, meaning that God knows of it because it will happen, even though His foreknowledge is chronologically prior to the event.

A helpful way to understand this is by thinking of foreknowledge as a foreshadowing or a shadow of something yet to come. For instance, if you see someone's shadow around the corner of a building before you see the person, you know that the person is about to appear because of their shadow. However, the shadow does not dictate the person's existence; rather, the person casts the shadow. Similarly, God's foreknowledge is like the shadow of a future event. By observing this shadow, God knows the events that will transpire. But the shadow does not shape the reality; instead, the reality casts the shadow.

Thus, we should perceive God's foreknowledge as a foreshadowing of future events. It's important to note that just because God knows something will happen, it does not bias or eliminate the freedom of that event to occur. In fact, if the events were to unfold differently, God's foreknowledge would also differ.

An apt analogy for this is an infallible weather barometer. Whatever the barometer indicates, because it is infallible, you know what the weather will be like. However, the barometer does not control the weather; the weather determines the barometer's readings. In the same vein, God's foreknowledge is like an infallible barometer of the future. It allows Him to know what the future will be, but it does not restrict the future in any way. The future will unfold as the free moral agent wishes it to, and the barometer will accurately track whatever direction the future takes.

The scriptural examination of predestination and foreknowledge reveals a complex interplay between divine sovereignty and human freedom. While God's omniscience allows Him to know all future events, this knowledge does not negate human freedom or responsibility. The Scriptures affirm that human beings have the capacity to respond to God's call, make genuine choices, and thus play a significant role in their own salvation journey. This understanding respects both the sovereignty of God in His plan of redemption and the agency of human beings as they respond to His grace and truth.

Implications of Unconditional Election on Christian Faith

The doctrine of unconditional election, as posited by Calvinism, asserts that God has predestined certain individuals to salvation regardless of their actions or choices. This view contrasts with the belief that human beings have the ability to respond to God's call and that their decisions can influence their salvation. Examining the implications of unconditional election on Christian faith sheds light on crucial theological and practical aspects of the doctrine of salvation.

1. The Nature of God's Sovereignty and Human Responsibility

Unconditional election places a strong emphasis on God's sovereignty, affirming that God's will is the ultimate determining factor in salvation. However, this can lead to questions regarding human responsibility and freedom.

- If God has predestined certain individuals to salvation, it raises questions about the role of human response, repentance, and faith. This could potentially diminish the importance of moral responsibility and decision-making in the Christian life.

- The Bible presents a view of God who desires all to be saved and who calls individuals to respond to His grace (1 Timothy 2:4; 2 Peter 3:9). This universal call seems inconsistent with the idea that salvation is limited to a predestined few.

2. The Concept of Justice and the Character of God

The doctrine of unconditional election can also raise concerns regarding the justice and character of God.

- If individuals are predestined to salvation or damnation without regard to their choices or actions, it may seem to conflict with the biblical portrayal of God as just and loving.

- Scriptures such as Ezekiel 18:23 and 33:11, where God expresses no pleasure in the death of the wicked but desires their repentance, suggest a divine character that is at odds with unconditional predestination.

3. Evangelism and the Great Commission

Unconditional election can influence the understanding and practice of evangelism and mission work.

- If the elect are predestined, it could lead to a passive approach to evangelism, under the belief that the elect will be saved regardless of human effort.

- However, the New Testament emphasizes active evangelism and the proclamation of the gospel to all nations (Matthew 28:19-20; Acts 1:8). This mandate suggests that human participation in spreading the gospel is vital.

4. Assurance of Salvation

The doctrine of unconditional election impacts the believer's assurance of salvation.

- Calvinism's teaching of the perseverance of the saints offers assurance to the elect that they cannot lose their salvation. However, it can also lead to anxiety about one's election status, as the certainty of being among the elect can be unclear.

- The biblical call to "make your calling and election sure" (2 Peter 1:10) and to "work out your salvation with fear and trembling" (Philippians 2:12) implies a more dynamic process, where assurance comes through a lived faith and ongoing relationship with God.

5. The Problem of Apostasy and Perseverance

Unconditional election poses challenges to understanding apostasy and perseverance in the faith.

- The possibility of apostasy, as warned in Hebrews 6:4-6 and 2 Peter 2:20-22, seems to contradict the idea of irrevocable election. If salvation can be lost through apostasy, then election cannot be entirely unconditional.

- The biblical exhortations to persevere in faith and obedience suggest that continued faithfulness is essential for maintaining one's relationship with God.

6. The Role of Faith and Works in Salvation

The interplay of faith and works in salvation is viewed differently under the lens of unconditional election.

- While unconditional election emphasizes God's grace as the sole basis of salvation, the Bible often links salvation with a faith that manifests in actions (James 2:14-26).

- Understanding salvation as a cooperative process involving God's grace and human response in faith and obedience provides a more holistic view of the Christian life.

7. Understanding Foreknowledge and Predestination

The biblical concept of foreknowledge, as articulated in Romans 8:29 and 1 Peter 1:2, needs to be reconciled with the notion of predestination.

- The idea that God's foreknowledge of future events, including human decisions, does not causally determine those events, maintains the compatibility between divine sovereignty and human freedom.

- This understanding sees God's foreknowledge as akin to an infallible barometer, indicating what will happen without constraining or compelling it, thus preserving human freedom.

Conclusion

The doctrine of unconditional election, when examined in light of Scripture, raises significant theological and practical concerns for Christian faith. A balanced view, which acknowledges both divine sovereignty and human responsibility, seems more consistent with the broader scriptural narrative. This perspective maintains that while God's grace initiates and enables salvation, human beings are called to respond in faith and obedience, participating actively in their salvation journey. This approach not only honors the sovereignty of God but also affirms the dignity and responsibility of human beings as moral agents created in the image of God.

Edward D. Andrews

APPENDIX C: Refuting Limited Atonement: The Scope of Christ's Sacrifice

Limited Atonement in Calvinist Doctrine

Limited Atonement is a doctrine in Calvinism that is closely tied to the Calvinist view of predestination and the nature of the atonement. This doctrine is part of the five points of Calvinism, often represented by the acronym TULIP, and is considered the most controversial among them.

The doctrine of Limited Atonement, also referred to as Particular Redemption or Definite Atonement, asserts that Jesus died on the cross to atone only for the sins of the elect, those predestined for salvation.

This doctrine does not limit the power of the atonement in any way, meaning no sin is too great to be expiated. It is called 'limited' because it effects salvation only for the elect, and 'definite' because it certainly secures the salvation of those for whom Christ died.

The doctrine of Limited Atonement is primarily concerned with the original purpose, plan, or design of God in sending Christ into the world to die on the cross 2. It questions whether God's intent was to make salvation possible for everyone or if He had a specific plan of salvation to ensure the salvation of His people.

While the death of Christ was sufficient to atone for the sins of the whole world, it was God's will that it should effectively redeem those and only those who were chosen from eternity and given to Christ by the Father. This belief empowers evangelism, resting on the understanding that the power of salvation is not in our presentation of the gospel or in the audience's ability to understand or desire to believe it, but rests solely upon an all-powerful God who has determined to save people from every tribe, tongue, and nation.

Scriptural Evidence for Universal Atonement [Not Universal Salvation]

The doctrine of limited atonement, as espoused in Calvinistic theology, contends that Christ's atoning sacrifice was intended only for the elect. However, a thorough examination of the Scriptures reveals a contrasting view: the universality of Christ's atonement. This understanding aligns with the belief that while salvation is offered to all, it is only actualized by those who choose to embrace it through faith.

The Universal Need for Atonement

The universality of sin establishes the need for a universal atonement. Scriptures like Romans 3:23, which states, "for all have sinned and fall short of the glory of God," indicate the universal nature of sin. The inherited sin from Adam, as delineated in Romans 5:12, underscores that all humanity is in need of redemption.

The Universality of God's Love

A foundational aspect of the doctrine of universal atonement is the universality of God's love. John 3:16 states, "For God so loved the world that he gave his only Son, that whoever believes in him should not perish but have eternal life." This verse does not limit God's love to a select group but extends it to the entire world, emphasizing the potential for salvation for all who believe.

The Sufficiency of Christ's Sacrifice

The New Testament presents Christ's sacrifice as sufficient for all. In 1 John 2:2, it is written, "He is the propitiation for our sins, and not for ours only but also for the sins of the whole world." This indicates that Christ's atoning work is not limited but is sufficiently comprehensive to cover the sins of the entire world.

The Offer of Salvation to All

The scriptural narrative consistently offers salvation to all. Acts 2:21 declares, "And it shall come to pass that everyone who calls upon the name of the Lord shall be saved." Such passages do not suggest a limitation on who can be saved but rather an open invitation to all.

The Nature of God's Foreknowledge

Understanding God's foreknowledge is crucial in this context. It is not about predestination in the Calvinistic sense but about God's comprehensive awareness of all potentialities. This foreknowledge does not negate human free will or the genuine offer of salvation to all.

The Old Testament Sacrificial System as a Foreshadowing of Christ's Atonement

The Old Testament sacrificial system, with special emphasis on the Day of Atonement as detailed in Leviticus 16, serves as a foreshadowing of the atoning work of Christ. These sacrifices, though temporary and imperfect, were offered for the benefit of all Israelites, reflecting a principle of inclusivity. This aspect of the Old Testament law highlights the comprehensive scope of Christ's future sacrifice, intended to extend its redemptive power to all humanity, not just a select few.

Christ's Role as the Second Adam

In 1 Corinthians 15:22, "For as in Adam all die, so also in Christ shall all be made alive," the apostle Paul presents Christ as the Second Adam. Just as Adam's act had universal implications for humanity, so too does Christ's atoning act have the potential for universal redemption.

The Open Invitation of the Gospel Call

The Great Commission (Matthew 28:19-20) and the universal call to repentance (Acts 17:30) further underscore the universality of Christ's atonement. These passages command the disciples to preach to all nations and people, suggesting the universal scope of the Gospel.

The Condemnation of Rejecting Christ

Hebrews 10:26-31 warns about the severity of rejecting Christ's sacrifice, suggesting that the offer of atonement is universal but can be rejected. This rejection results in the loss of the opportunity for salvation, a choice made by individuals rather than a predestined condition.

The doctrine of universal atonement is deeply rooted in the Scripture's portrayal of God's love, the nature of Christ's sacrifice, and the universal need for redemption. It presents a God who desires all to be saved (1 Timothy 2:4) and who has provided a means of salvation through Jesus Christ for every person. This belief does not endorse universal salvation but upholds the necessity of personal faith and repentance for salvation. The scriptural evidence suggests an atonement that is universally sufficient and potentially effective for all, yet it is only actualized in those who choose to embrace it.

The Open Invitation of Christ's Redemptive Work

Christ's redemptive work, as delineated in the Scriptures, is a pivotal aspect of Christian soteriology. This appendix addresses the concept of limited atonement, as posited in Calvinistic theology, and presents the scriptural basis for Christ's sacrificial act being an open invitation to all, rather than being restricted to a preselected few.

The All-Encompassing Nature of Sin and the Necessity for Atonement

The Bible clearly states that all humanity is affected by sin, necessitating a comprehensive solution. Romans 3:23, stating "for all have sinned and fall short of the glory of God," along with Romans 5:12, which speaks of the transmission of sin from Adam to all his descendants, underscores the need for a redemptive plan that is available to everyone.

The Extent of God's Love

The Scriptures reveal God's love as being extended to all of humanity. This is exemplified in John 3:16, which speaks of God's love for the world and His provision of His Son for the salvation of those who believe. This love is not restrictive but is an offer of redemption to everyone.

The Sufficiency of Christ's Sacrifice

In the New Testament, Christ's sacrifice is portrayed as not only effective but also as sufficient for the redemption of any who choose to embrace it through faith. 1 John 2:2, for instance, describes Christ as the propitiation for the sins of the whole world, indicating the broad scope of His atoning work.

The Open Invitation for Salvation

The offer of salvation through Christ is consistently presented in Scripture as open to all individuals. This is illustrated in verses like Acts 2:21, which proclaims that "everyone who calls on the name of the Lord shall be saved." This open invitation emphasizes the availability of salvation to every person.

Foreknowledge and Human Agency

God's foreknowledge, which includes awareness of all potential futures, does not negate human free will. This concept ensures that human decisions, particularly regarding the acceptance or rejection of Christ's offer of salvation, remain within the realm of personal choice and responsibility.

Christ as the Antitype of Old Testament Sacrifices

The Old Testament sacrificial system, especially as seen in the Day of Atonement, serves as a precursor to understanding the complete work of Christ. These sacrifices, while temporary and imperfect, were for the benefit of all Israel, pointing towards the complete and perfect sacrifice of Christ, intended for the benefit of all who would believe.

The Role of Christ as the Perfect Sacrifice

Christ, as the sinless sacrifice (2 Corinthians 5:21), uniquely fulfills the requirements for atonement. His offering, unlike any other, was adequate for the sins of any individual, perfectly bridging the gap caused by sin.

Reconciliation Through Christ

The alienation caused by sin between humanity and God can only be remedied through Christ's atoning work. Passages such as Romans 5:11 illustrate the reconciliation that is now available through Jesus Christ. This reconciliation is not automatically applied to all but is accessible to those who choose to accept it through faith.

Christ's Sacrifice: A Call for Faithful Response

The sacrifice of Christ calls for a response of faith and repentance. This response is crucial for individuals to benefit from Christ's atoning work. Scriptures such as Romans 3:21-26 highlight the necessity of faith in Christ for the realization of salvation.

The Consequences of Rejecting Christ

Scripture warns of the serious consequences of rejecting Christ's sacrifice, as seen in Hebrews 10:26-31. This warning underscores the importance of individual decision in the matter of salvation, indicating that the opportunity for redemption, while offered to all, can be forfeited through unbelief or rejection.

The scriptural evidence supports the view that Christ's redemptive work is an open invitation to salvation, offered to all individuals without discrimination. This view respects the free will of each person in accepting or rejecting this offer and underscores the comprehensive nature of Christ's sacrifice, sufficient to atone for the sins of any who choose to believe.

Analyzing Key Passages on the Opportunity of Salvation for All

The doctrine of salvation, especially as it pertains to the atoning work of Christ, is a cornerstone of Christian faith. In this appendix, I address the concept of limited atonement and present a scriptural analysis to affirm that Christ's sacrifice provides the opportunity for salvation to all individuals, not just a predestined few. This perspective aligns with a literal and historical-grammatical interpretation of the Scriptures.

The Biblical Basis of Atonement

The concept of atonement, rooted in the idea of sin covering or reconciliation, is foundational in understanding Christ's work. Atonement, as per the Old Testament (Hebrew Scriptures), involved the covering of sins (Leviticus and Numbers). The Hebrew term 'Ka·phar" suggests a covering or wiping off of sins. In the context of humanity's inherited sin from Adam (Romans 5:12), atonement is necessary for the restoration of the relationship between God and man, fractured due to sin.

The Need for a Perfect Sacrifice

The Old Testament sacrificial system, while symbolically significant, was inadequate for the complete remission of sins, as animals are inferior to humans. This inadequacy pointed to the need for a perfect sacrifice, fulfilled in Jesus Christ (Hebrews 10:1-4). Jesus' sinless life and sacrificial death provided the precise atonement required to cover humanity's sin, as stated in 2 Corinthians 5:21 and 1 Peter 2:24.

Christ's Sacrifice: An Offer of Salvation for All

Christ's sacrificial death on the cross was not limited to a select group but was intended as an offer of salvation for all who would believe. This is affirmed in John 3:16, which states God's love for the world and His desire for all to attain eternal life through faith in His Son.

Key Scriptural Passages

1. **1 Timothy 2:5-6**: This passage highlights Jesus as the mediator for all, stating that He gave Himself as a ransom for all. This indicates the potential for salvation to every individual, not just a preselected few.

2. **2 Peter 3:9**: Peter emphasizes that God is patient, "not wanting anyone to perish, but everyone to come to repentance." This verse suggests God's desire for all to have the opportunity for salvation.

3. **Hebrews 2:9**: This verse indicates that Jesus tasted death for everyone, further supporting the view that His atoning sacrifice was intended for all of humanity.

4. **Romans 5:18**: Paul explains that just as Adam's trespass led to condemnation for all men, so Christ's act of righteousness leads to justification and life for all men. This parallel between Adam and Christ emphasizes the comprehensive impact of Christ's redemptive work.

The Role of Faith and Repentance

While Christ's sacrifice provides the opportunity for salvation to all, it requires an individual response of faith and repentance. This concept is supported by Romans 10:13, which promises salvation to everyone who calls on the name of the Lord. Faith and repentance are essential in actualizing the potential of Christ's atonement in an individual's life.

A thorough analysis of the Scriptures reveals that Christ's atoning sacrifice was not limited to a select few but was an offer of salvation extended to all individuals. This view upholds the principles of God's justice and love, providing a way for reconciliation through faith in Jesus Christ. The opportunity for salvation, therefore, is open to all, contingent upon personal faith and repentance, aligning with the core tenets of biblical, Christian theology.

Limited Atonement and the Character of God

The doctrine of limited atonement, as part of the Calvinistic TULIP theology, proposes that Christ's atoning sacrifice was intended exclusively for the elect and not for all of humanity. This perspective, however, raises significant questions about the character of God as revealed in the Scriptures. As a biblically minded person, it is essential to examine this doctrine in light of the Biblical portrayal of God's nature, justice, love, and the provision of salvation.

God's Nature and Justice

The nature of God, as depicted in the Bible, is intrinsically linked to His attributes of justice and righteousness. The Old Testament frequently emphasizes God's just character (Deuteronomy 32:4). In this light, the concept of limited atonement seems to contradict the Biblical portrayal of a just God who "does not show partiality nor take a bribe" (2 Chronicles 19:7).

Justice, in the Biblical sense, requires that all individuals have the opportunity for salvation. The idea that Christ's sacrifice was limited to a preselected group undermines the impartiality of divine justice. It suggests a scenario where many are condemned without any real opportunity for redemption, a concept that seems inconsistent with the Biblical depiction of God's justice.

God's Love and Mercy

The Bible extensively proclaims God's love and mercy towards humanity. John 3:16, one of the most cited verses, speaks of God's love for the world and His desire for everyone to have eternal life through faith in Jesus. Similarly, scriptures like 1 Timothy 2:4 express God's desire for all people to be saved.

Limited atonement conflicts with these declarations of God's love and desire for salvation to be available to all. The notion that Christ died only for a select few seems to limit God's love, contradicting passages that affirm His love for the whole world.

The Sacrifice of Christ

The New Testament presents Christ's sacrifice as a pivotal event for humanity's redemption. Passages like 1 John 2:2, where Christ is described as the propitiation for the sins of the whole world, indicate the broad scope of His atonement. Similarly, Hebrews 2:9 states that Jesus tasted death for everyone, further emphasizing the extensive reach of His sacrificial act.

In the context of limited atonement, these verses pose a theological challenge. If Christ's sacrifice was only for the elect, then such declarations in the New Testament would be misleading or incorrect.

Human Freedom and Divine Foreknowledge

The Bible acknowledges human freedom and responsibility in the context of salvation. Verses like Romans 10:13, which promises salvation to all who call on the Lord, suggest that individual choice plays a role in receiving salvation. This perspective aligns with the view that God's foreknowledge does not dictate human choices but rather foresees them in a way that does not compromise human freedom.

Limited atonement implies a deterministic framework where human response is irrelevant for salvation, as the outcome is predetermined. This view is hard to reconcile with the scriptural emphasis on repentance, faith, and the personal acceptance of Christ's sacrifice.

In conclusion, the doctrine of limited atonement raises significant concerns when examined in light of the Biblical portrayal of God's character. The scriptural evidence of God's justice, love, the extensive scope of Christ's sacrifice, and the role of human freedom in salvation challenges the notion that Christ's atoning work was intended for a limited group.

The Biblical depiction of a just and loving God, who desires the opportunity for salvation to be available to all, seems to be more consistent with a view that Christ's sacrifice was sufficient for all and potentially effective for anyone who chooses to believe. This perspective not only aligns with the core attributes of God as revealed in the Scriptures but also respects the principles of divine justice and love, providing a more coherent theological framework for understanding the scope of Christ's sacrifice.

Edward D. Andrews

APPENDIX D: Irresistible Grace: An Analysis and Response

The Doctrine of Irresistible Grace in Calvinism

Irresistible Grace, also known as effectual grace or effectual calling, is a key doctrine in Calvinism. This doctrine asserts that God's saving grace is effectively applied to those whom He has chosen to save (the elect) and, at the right time, overcomes their resistance to obeying the call of the gospel, leading them to faith in Christ.

The term "irresistible" in this context does not imply that God's grace cannot be resisted at all. Instead, it means that when God chooses to save someone, His grace will ultimately overcome any resistance, leading to the person's salvation.

This doctrine is distinct from the concept of prevenient grace, which is associated with Arminianism. Prevenient grace suggests that the offer of salvation through grace does not act irresistibly in a purely cause-effect, deterministic method, but rather in an influence-and-response fashion that can be both freely accepted and freely denied.

The doctrine of Irresistible Grace emphasizes that God must initiate the work of salvation because human wills are inherently set against Him and cannot turn towards Him on their own. This belief underscores the sovereignty of God in the process of salvation, asserting that the power of salvation rests solely upon an all-powerful God who has determined to save people from every tribe, tongue, and nation.

Biblical Examples of Resisted Grace

The doctrine of Irresistible Grace, as a component of Calvinism's TULIP theology, posits that those elected by God for salvation cannot resist His grace. However, this viewpoint raises significant theological and scriptural questions, especially when examined in light of numerous Biblical accounts where individuals seemingly resist God's grace. It is essential to analyze these instances to provide a comprehensive understanding of the dynamic between divine grace and human free will.

The Nature of Grace in the Bible

Grace, as presented in the Bible, is the unmerited favor of God toward humanity. It is fundamental to understanding God's interaction with humanity, especially in the context of salvation. The offer of grace, while sovereignly initiated by God, involves human response, suggesting that grace can be accepted or rejected.

Old Testament Instances of Resisted Grace

1. **Pharaoh in Exodus**: The story of Pharaoh (Exodus 7-14) is a prime example. Despite witnessing numerous miracles and plagues that should have led to recognition of God's power, Pharaoh repeatedly hardens his heart, resisting God's grace and will.

2. **Israelites in the Wilderness**: The Israelites frequently resisted God's guidance and provision in the wilderness (Numbers 14:11). Despite witnessing miraculous deliverance from Egypt and continuous provision, they grumbled and turned away from God multiple times, indicating resistance to His grace.

3. **Saul, the First King of Israel**: Saul's reign as detailed in 1 Samuel 15 is another example. Despite being chosen by God and given specific instructions, Saul disobeys God, indicating a rejection of divine grace and guidance.

New Testament Instances of Resisted Grace

1. **Judas Iscariot**: As one of the twelve disciples, Judas experienced Christ's teachings and miracles firsthand (Matthew 26:14-16, 47-50; 27:3-5). Despite this, he chose to betray Jesus, demonstrating a clear instance of resisting grace.

2. **Religious Leaders in the Gospels**: The Pharisees and religious leaders, despite witnessing Jesus'

miracles and hearing His teachings, often resisted and rejected His message (Matthew 12:24, John 11:47-53). This resistance illustrates their refusal to accept the grace manifested in Christ.

3. **The Rich Young Ruler**: In Mark 10:17-22, the rich young ruler, upon being offered eternal life by Jesus, chooses his wealth over following Christ, illustrating a resistance to the grace offered by Jesus.

Theological Implications

These Biblical examples challenge the concept of Irresistible Grace. They demonstrate that while God's grace is freely extended, it can indeed be resisted and rejected. This resistance does not imply a limitation in God's power or grace but rather highlights the role of human free will in the process of salvation.

The doctrine of Irresistible Grace seems to negate the personal responsibility emphasized in the Bible. Scriptures like Revelation 3:20, where Jesus says, "Behold, I stand at the door and knock. If anyone hears My voice and opens the door, I will come in to him," suggest an element of human choice in responding to God's grace.

While God's grace is a powerful force that brings many to salvation, the Biblical narrative provides numerous examples where individuals resist this grace. These instances suggest that the acceptance of divine grace is not an automatic or irresistible process but involves a human response. This perspective aligns more closely with the Biblical portrayal of a God who respects human freedom while sovereignly extending His grace to humanity. The balance between divine sovereignty and human responsibility remains a profound mystery, but the scriptural evidence seems to favor a view that allows for the possibility of resisting God's grace.

The Dynamics of Divine Grace and Human Agency

In Christian theology, the relationship between divine grace and human agency is a complex and often debated topic. This analysis aims to explore the dynamics of this relationship, particularly in the context of salvation, and provide a response to the doctrine of Irresistible Grace as proposed in Calvinistic theology.

Understanding Divine Grace

Grace, in Christian doctrine, is understood as the unmerited favor of God towards humanity. It is an expression of His love and mercy, independent of human worthiness. Grace is central to the Christian understanding of salvation, as it is through grace that individuals are saved (Ephesians 2:8-9).

The Concept of Irresistible Grace in Calvinism

Irresistible Grace, a tenet of Calvinism, asserts that the grace extended by God for salvation cannot be resisted by those whom He has elected. According to this doctrine, those chosen by God will inevitably come to faith, as the grace extended to them is overpowering and inevitable in its effect.

Biblical Analysis of Human Agency

The Bible presents numerous instances where human responses to God's initiatives play a crucial role. For example:

- **The Parable of the Sower** (Matthew 13:1-23): Jesus describes different responses to the word of God, indicating that the reception of divine truth varies among individuals, suggesting the presence of human agency.

- **Stephen's Address** (Acts 7:51): Stephen accuses the Sanhedrin of resisting the Holy Spirit, indicating that resistance to God's grace is a possibility.

- **Paul's Epistles**: Paul often exhorts his readers to choose to live in a manner worthy of their calling (Ephesians 4:1), implying that human choices and actions are significant in response to divine grace.

Theological Implications of Irresistible Grace

The doctrine of Irresistible Grace raises questions about the nature of human freedom and responsibility. If grace is truly irresistible, it implies that human response is irrelevant, which seems to contradict the Biblical emphasis on personal repentance and faith. This view can also lead to a deterministic understanding of salvation, potentially negating the need for evangelism and personal transformation.

Counter-Arguments to Irresistible Grace

1. **God's Universal Call**: Scriptures like 1 Timothy 2:4, which states that God desires all people to be saved, suggest that His grace is extended universally, not limited to a select few.

2. **Human Response**: The consistent Biblical call for repentance and faith (Acts 17:30, Romans 10:9-10) implies that human beings have a role in responding to God's grace.

3. **Examples of Resistance**: As previously mentioned, instances of individuals resisting God's call, like in Stephen's address, indicate that while God's grace is powerful and transformative, it can be resisted.

The Balance Between Divine Sovereignty and Human Responsibility

A balanced theological perspective acknowledges both divine sovereignty and human responsibility. While God in His sovereignty initiates salvation through grace, human beings are responsible for their response to this grace. This balance respects the mystery of God's providential work while affirming the Biblical call to faith and repentance.

While the doctrine of Irresistible Grace emphasizes the efficacy of God's grace in salvation, a comprehensive analysis of the Scriptures suggests a more nuanced relationship between divine grace and human agency. The Biblical narrative and doctrinal understanding of grace as seen in Christian tradition support the view that human beings, while completely dependent on God's grace for salvation, are also active participants in responding to this grace. This perspective upholds the integrity of human freedom, the universal call to salvation, and the personal nature of faith, all of which are essential components of the Christian faith.

Grace, Faith, and the Call to Repentance

In Christian theology, the concepts of grace, faith, and repentance are fundamental to understanding the doctrine of salvation. This analysis delves into the intricate relationship between these elements, particularly in light of the debate surrounding the doctrine of Irresistible Grace as proposed in Calvinistic theology.

The Nature of Divine Grace

Grace is central to Christian soteriology. It is God's unmerited favor and lovingkindness toward humanity, a gift that cannot be earned by human efforts (Ephesians 2:8-9). Grace is the divine initiative in the salvation of sinners, an expression of God's love and mercy.

The Role of Faith in Salvation

Faith is the human response to God's grace. It is more than intellectual assent; it is a trustful surrender to God and a firm belief in His promises, particularly the redemptive work of Jesus Christ (Hebrews 11:1). Faith is the means by which individuals receive the grace offered by God.

Edward D. Andrews

Repentance: A Necessary Response to Grace

Repentance is a crucial aspect of the Christian journey toward salvation. It involves a heartfelt sorrow for sin, a turning away from sinfulness, and a sincere commitment to walk in obedience to God's commandments (Acts 3:19). Repentance is evidence of the transformative power of grace in an individual's life.

Examining the Doctrine of Irresistible Grace

Irresistible Grace, as posited in Calvinism, asserts that God's grace is effective to the point of being irresistible to the elect. According to this view, those whom God has chosen for salvation will inevitably come to faith, as they cannot resist God's grace.

Biblical Instances Suggesting Resistible Grace

The Bible presents several instances where individuals resist God's call and grace:

1. **Pharaoh in the Exodus Account**: Despite witnessing numerous signs and wonders, Pharaoh repeatedly hardens his heart, resisting God's call to let the Israelites go (Exodus 7-14).

2. **Israelites' Rebellion**: The Israelites, despite experiencing God's miraculous deliverance and provision, repeatedly rebelled against God in the wilderness (Numbers 14).

3. **New Testament Warnings**: The New Testament contains warnings against falling away from faith

(Hebrews 6:4-6), suggesting that resisting grace is a real possibility for believers.

The Balance between Divine Sovereignty and Human Responsibility

While God's sovereignty in salvation is a biblical truth, it does not negate human responsibility. The call to repentance and faith implies a human response to God's grace. Scriptures affirm both divine initiative in salvation and human responsibility to respond in faith and repentance.

Theological Implications

1. **God's Sovereign Call and Human Freedom**: The doctrine of salvation must account for both God's sovereign calling and human freedom. While God initiates salvation through grace, individuals are called to respond in faith and repentance.

2. **The Purpose of Evangelism**: The call to evangelism and the Great Commission (Matthew 28:19-20) imply that human beings can respond to God's grace. The effort put into evangelism and missions aligns with the belief that individuals can accept or reject God's offer of salvation.

3. **Apostasy and Perseverance**: The possibility of apostasy and the need for perseverance in faith (2 Peter 2:20-22) suggest that grace can be resisted and that continued faith is essential for final salvation.

While grace is a gift from God and a demonstration of His sovereign love, the Bible suggests that it requires a human response of faith and repentance. The evidence of resistible grace in Scripture challenges the doctrine of Irresistible Grace and upholds the dynamic interplay between divine grace and human agency. This perspective maintains the integrity of human freedom, the seriousness of the call to repentance, and the personal nature of faith, all of which are vital elements in the Christian understanding of salvation.

Reconciling God's Grace with Human Freedom

The theological discourse surrounding God's grace and human freedom is complex and multifaceted, especially when considering the doctrine of Irresistible Grace within Calvinism. This appendix explores how God's grace operates in tandem with human freedom, addressing the nuances of this relationship in light of scriptural teachings and theological principles.

Understanding Divine Grace

Divine grace is central to Christian theology, representing God's unmerited favor towards humanity. It is through grace that salvation is offered, a gift that cannot be earned by human works (Ephesians 2:8-9). This grace is manifested in the person and work of Jesus Christ, offering redemption and reconciliation to all who believe.

The Doctrine of Irresistible Grace

Irresistible Grace, a pillar of Calvinistic theology, suggests that the saving grace of God is effectually applied to those whom He has determined to save (the elect) and, consequently, cannot be resisted. This doctrine posits that

God's grace inevitably results in the salvation of the intended recipient.

The Role of Human Freedom

The concept of human freedom, particularly in accepting or rejecting salvation, is a critical aspect of Christian belief. The Bible presents numerous instances where individuals are called to respond to God's initiative, implying the existence of free will. For example, Revelation 3:20 depicts Jesus as standing at the door and knocking, suggesting that the individual has the freedom to open the door.

Scriptural Instances Suggesting Resistible Grace

Several biblical narratives and teachings suggest that grace can be resisted:

1. **Stephen's Rebuke**: In Acts 7:51, Stephen accuses his listeners of resisting the Holy Spirit, indicating that resistance to God's will and grace is possible.

2. **Parable of the Sower**: Jesus' parable in Matthew 13:1-23 illustrates different responses to the word of God, suggesting that human reception of divine grace varies.

3. **Warnings against Falling Away**: The New Testament contains admonitions against falling away from the faith (Hebrews 6:4-6, 2 Peter 2:20-22), implying that believers can resist or turn away from grace.

Balancing Divine Sovereignty and Human Responsibility

Reconciling God's sovereignty with human free will is a complex theological endeavor. While God is sovereign and initiates salvation, human beings are called to respond to His grace. This dynamic does not diminish God's sovereignty but acknowledges human agency as part of God's redemptive plan.

Theological Implications

1. **God's Sovereign Call and Human Response**: The interplay between God's sovereign call and human response is essential in understanding salvation. While God extends grace, the individual's response of faith and repentance plays a vital role.

2. **The Purpose of Evangelism**: The emphasis on evangelism and preaching the Gospel underscores the belief in human capacity to respond to God's grace. If grace were truly irresistible, the imperative to evangelize would lose its urgency.

3. **The Nature of Apostasy**: The possibility of apostasy, where a believer falls away from faith, suggests that grace requires continual response and nurturing through faith and obedience.

Conclusion

In conclusion, the doctrine of Irresistible Grace, when closely examined in the light of scripture, raises significant questions about the nature of human freedom and the character of God. The scriptural evidence points towards a model where divine grace and human response coexist within the framework of God's sovereign plan of salvation. This model upholds the integrity of human freedom, the necessity of a personal response to God's grace, and the continuous nature of faith, aligning with the broader scriptural narrative of a loving God who desires a relationship with His creation.

Edward D. Andrews

APPENDIX E: The Perseverance of the Saints: A Critical Review

Understanding Perseverance of the Saints in Calvinist Thought

The doctrine of Perseverance of the Saints is a fundamental tenet in Calvinist theology. It is part of the five points of Calvinism, often represented by the acronym TULIP. This doctrine addresses the question of the eternal security of the believer, asking: "Once a person is saved, can he lose his salvation?"

Perseverance of the Saints suggests that those who are truly saved will persevere to the end and cannot lose their salvation. This is because God, in His sovereignty, will ensure the preservation of the saints. However, it's important to note that this doctrine does not mean that the journey of faith will be without struggles or serious measures of unbelief.

The term "perseverance" can sometimes be misleading, as it might suggest that the perseverance is something that we do, perhaps in and of ourselves. Therefore, some people prefer to use terms like "preservation of the saints" or "eternal security", which emphasize that the process by which we are kept in a state of grace is something that is accomplished by God.

While the doctrine of Perseverance of the Saints asserts the eternal security of the believer, it also emphasizes that the saints will and must persevere in faith and the obedience which comes from faith. There are many warnings in Scripture that those who do not hold fast to Christ can be lost in the end. Therefore, while election is unconditional, glorification is not.

Scriptural Evidence for Conditional Security

The doctrine of the Perseverance of the Saints, a key tenet of Calvinism, posits that those truly regenerated and saved will inevitably persevere in faith until the end. However, a critical examination of scriptural evidence reveals numerous instances where salvation is depicted as conditional, contingent on continued faith, obedience, and discipleship. This perspective aligns with the belief that a genuine Christian can fall away from the faith and lose their salvation, emphasizing the dynamic nature of the Christian journey.

The Conditional Nature of Discipleship and Salvation

The New Testament contains several conditional statements that suggest the security of a believer is contingent upon certain criteria:

1. **John 15:6 - Abiding in Christ**: Jesus states, "If anyone does not abide in Me, he is thrown away as a branch and withers; and the branches are gathered, thrown into the fire, and burned." This metaphor emphasizes the necessity of continuing in faith and communion with Christ.

2. **Matthew 7:21 - Doing the Father's Will**: "Not everyone who says to Me, 'Lord, Lord,' will enter the kingdom of heaven, but the one who does the will of My Father who is in heaven." Here, Jesus highlights that mere verbal profession is not enough; doing God's will is crucial.

3. **Hebrews 10:26-27 - The Danger of Willful Sin**: "For if we go on sinning deliberately after receiving the knowledge of the truth, there no longer remains a sacrifice for sins, but a fearful expectation of judgment..." This passage warns of the severe consequences of turning away from the path of righteousness.

4. **2 Peter 2:20-22 - The Peril of Turning Away**: "For if, after they have escaped the defilements of the world through the knowledge of our Lord and Savior Jesus Christ, they are again entangled in them and overcome, the last state has become worse for them than the first." This text suggests that it is possible for believers to fall away and face worse outcomes.

5. **Revelation 3:5 - Overcoming**: "The one who conquers will be clothed thus in white garments, and I will never blot his name out of the book of life." The implication is that perseverance in faith is necessary for the assurance of salvation.

The Role of Human Agency in Salvation

While God's grace initiates and sustains salvation, human response and cooperation are consistently emphasized in Scripture. The call to repentance, faith, and obedience indicates that believers play an active role in their salvation journey.

The Concept of Apostasy

The New Testament addresses the concept of apostasy, where a believer can turn away from the faith. This turning away is not merely backsliding but a willful rejection of Christ and His teachings, leading to a state where repentance becomes increasingly difficult, if not impossible (Hebrews 6:4-6).

Reconciling Divine Sovereignty and Human Responsibility

The challenge lies in reconciling God's sovereignty with human responsibility. While God is sovereign in the work of salvation, He has also granted human beings free will to accept or reject His grace. This dynamic does not undermine God's sovereignty but rather highlights the relational aspect of salvation.

Theological Implications of Conditional Security

1. **The Need for Perseverance**: The conditional nature of salvation underscores the need for believers to persevere in faith and obedience. This perseverance is both a response to God's grace and a part of the sanctification process.

2. **The Role of the Church**: The church plays a vital role in encouraging and admonishing believers to continue in the faith, providing support, teaching, and accountability.

3. **The Assurance of Salvation**: While salvation is conditional, it is not insecure. Believers can have assurance of their salvation as they continue to walk in faith and obedience, relying on God's grace.

The scriptural evidence suggests that the security of a believer in Christ is conditional, dependent on continued faith, obedience, and abiding in Christ. This perspective respects the balance between divine sovereignty and human responsibility, emphasizing the dynamic nature of the Christian life. It calls for a diligent and faithful response to God's grace, fostering a deeper commitment to Christ and His teachings.

The Continual Call to Faithfulness and Obedience

The doctrine of the Perseverance of the Saints, central to Calvinistic theology, holds that those truly saved will inevitably persist in faith. However, a critical examination of the Scriptures reveals a consistent theme: the call to continual faithfulness and obedience, which suggests that perseverance in faith is not automatic but requires active participation by believers. This view aligns with the belief that Christians can fall away from their faith and underscores the dynamic nature of the Christian life.

The Biblical Emphasis on Obedience and Perseverance

1. **Conditional Promises in Scripture**: The Bible contains numerous instances where God's promises are contingent upon obedience and faithfulness. For instance, in John 15:4-6, Jesus emphasizes the need to "abide" in Him, warning that those who do not remain in Him will be like branches that are thrown away and wither.

2. **The Warnings Against Apostasy**: Scripture repeatedly warns against falling away from the faith. Hebrews 6:4-6 speaks of the impossibility of restoring those who have once been enlightened and then have fallen away, indicating that apostasy is a real danger for believers.

3. **The Call to Endurance**: The New Testament frequently exhorts believers to endure. In Matthew 24:13, Jesus says, "But the one who endures to the end will be saved," highlighting the necessity of enduring faith.

4. **The Role of Human Agency in Salvation**: While salvation is initiated by God's grace, human response is crucial. Verses like Philippians 2:12, which instructs believers to "work out your own salvation with fear and trembling," suggest an active role for believers in their spiritual journey.

Theological Implications of Conditional Perseverance

1. **Human Responsibility in Salvation**: This perspective emphasizes human responsibility in the process of salvation. It acknowledges that while God's grace is essential, human beings must respond to that grace through ongoing faith and obedience.

2. **The Role of Faith and Works**: The relationship between faith and works is a complex but crucial aspect of this discussion. James 2:26 notes that "faith without works is dead," suggesting that genuine faith is manifested in a life of obedience and good works.

3. **The Nature of True Faith**: True faith, according to this view, is not merely a one-time event but a continuous living relationship with God. It requires perseverance, growth in holiness, and ongoing trust in God.

4. **Assurance of Salvation**: The doctrine of conditional perseverance does not deny the assurance of salvation but frames it in the context of a faithful and obedient walk with God. Assurance is found not in a past decision but in a current and active relationship with Christ.

5. **Eternal Security vs. Assurance**: This perspective distinguishes between eternal security, seen as a potentially misleading concept that can lead to complacency, and assurance, which is a confident trust in God rooted in a life of ongoing faithfulness.

The scriptural evidence suggests that the perseverance of the saints is conditional, requiring continual faithfulness and obedience. This view upholds the sovereignty of God in salvation while emphasizing the crucial role of human response. It encourages believers to live out their faith actively and persistently, fostering a deeper commitment to Christ and His teachings. This approach to understanding salvation respects the balance between divine grace and human responsibility, ensuring a dynamic and transformative Christian journey.

Case Studies of Apostasy and Redemption in Scripture

The concept of apostasy, the act of falling away from faith, is a significant theological subject, particularly in the context of the perseverance of the saints. This critical review examines various scriptural narratives that illustrate instances of apostasy and redemption, offering insights into the dynamics of faith, perseverance, and the possibility of restoration.

Old Testament Examples

1. **King Saul (1 Samuel 15)**: Saul, initially chosen by God and anointed as king, disobeyed God's command. His refusal to fully obey God's instructions and his subsequent spiritual decline is a classic example of apostasy. Despite being anointed, Saul's actions demonstrate that continuous obedience and faith are crucial for maintaining one's standing before God.

2. **The Israelites (Exodus 32; Numbers 14)**: The Israelites frequently turned away from God, despite witnessing His miracles. The golden calf incident and their refusal to enter the Promised Land are

stark reminders of how even those who have experienced God's power can fall into unbelief and disobedience.

3. **King Solomon (1 Kings 11)**: Solomon, known for his wisdom, turned away from God in his later years by worshiping other gods, influenced by his foreign wives. His apostasy shows that even the wisest and most blessed individuals can fall away from their devotion to God.

New Testament Examples

1. **Judas Iscariot (Matthew 26:14-16, 47-50; 27:3-5)**: As one of the twelve disciples, Judas experienced Jesus' teachings and miracles firsthand. Yet, he chose to betray Jesus, a direct act of apostasy. His story highlights the sobering reality that proximity to Christ and knowledge of the truth does not guarantee perseverance in faith.

2. **Ananias and Sapphira (Acts 5:1-11)**: This couple, part of the early Christian community, lied to the Holy Spirit about the proceeds of a land sale. Their sudden deaths serve as a warning about the seriousness of sin and deceit within the church.

3. **Demas (2 Timothy 4:10)**: Demas, a co-worker of Paul, is mentioned as having loved this present world and therefore deserted Paul. This indicates that worldly attractions can lead to a departure from the faith.

Theological Reflections

1. **Human Agency and Divine Sovereignty**: These examples demonstrate the interaction of human

free will and divine sovereignty. While God's grace enables faith, individuals can choose to turn away from God, underscoring the importance of human agency in the perseverance of faith.

2. **The Call to Perseverance**: The Bible consistently calls believers to persevere in faith and obedience. This ongoing process involves daily commitment, prayer, and reliance on God's strength.

3. **The Possibility of Restoration**: Scripture also shows that restoration is possible for those who repent. King David's life (Psalm 51), after his serious transgressions, is an example of how genuine repentance can lead to restoration with God.

4. **Assurance of Salvation**: While these examples show that apostasy is a real possibility, they also underscore the assurance that can be found in a continued, faithful relationship with God. Believers can have confidence in their salvation as they persist in faith, rooted in the grace of God.

The scriptural narratives of apostasy and redemption illustrate the complex interplay between divine grace and human response. They serve as both warnings against complacency and assurances of God's willingness to restore those who return to Him in genuine repentance. These case studies underscore the need for continual faithfulness and reliance on God's sustaining grace in the Christian journey.

The Balance of Assurance and Diligence in Christian Life

In Christian theology, the doctrine of the Perseverance of the Saints, particularly as articulated in Calvinism, suggests that those truly regenerated cannot ultimately fall away from the state of grace. However, this doctrine needs careful examination, especially when considering the Biblical emphasis on both the assurance of salvation and the necessity for diligent perseverance in faith. This critical review explores the Biblical teachings on these aspects, considering the balance between assurance in Christ and the call for ongoing faithfulness and obedience.

The Assurance of Salvation

1. **Biblical Basis for Assurance**: The New Testament provides believers with assurances of their salvation. For instance, John 10:28-29 speaks of Jesus giving eternal life to His sheep, and no one can snatch them out of His hand. Similarly, Romans 8:38-39 assures believers that nothing can separate them from the love of God in Christ Jesus.

2. **Faith in Christ as the Foundation**: Assurance is based on faith in Christ's finished work on the cross and His resurrection, not on human merit (Ephesians 2:8-9). This assurance is a source of comfort and strength for believers, encouraging them in their walk with God.

3. **The Witness of the Holy Spirit**: Romans 8:16 indicates that the Holy Spirit testifies with our spirit that we are God's children, which is a key element of assurance. This inner witness contributes to the believer's confidence in their salvation.

The Call to Diligence and Perseverance

1. **Exhortations to Persevere**: The New Testament contains numerous exhortations to persevere in

faith and obedience. Hebrews 10:36, for instance, urges believers to persevere so that after they have done the will of God, they will receive what is promised.

2. **Warnings Against Apostasy**: The possibility of falling away from faith is a recurring theme. Hebrews 6:4-6 warns about the danger and consequences of falling away, suggesting that continued faithfulness is essential.

3. **The Role of Works in Faith**: While salvation is not by works, genuine faith is evidenced by works (James 2:26). These works are not the basis of salvation but rather the fruit of a living and active faith.

Reconciling Assurance and Diligence

1. **Divine Sovereignty and Human Responsibility**: This balance reflects the Biblical tension between God's sovereignty in salvation and human responsibility. Believers are secure in Christ, yet they are called to live out their faith actively.

2. **The Dynamic Nature of Faith**: Faith is not static; it involves a dynamic relationship with God. This relationship is nurtured through prayer, worship, obedience, and continual reliance on God's grace.

3. **The Purpose of Warnings**: Scriptural warnings serve as means by which God keeps His people on the path of faith. They remind believers of the seriousness of their commitment to Christ and the need for continual growth and vigilance.

4. **Assurance as Motivation for Obedience**: Assurance should not lead to complacency.

Instead, it serves as a motivation for obedience, knowing that believers' efforts are not in vain in the Lord (1 Corinthians 15:58).

Conclusion

In conclusion, the doctrine of the Perseverance of the Saints must be understood in light of the entire scriptural teaching on salvation. While believers can have assurance in their relationship with Christ, this assurance coexists with a clear Biblical mandate for ongoing diligence and faithfulness. This balanced perspective encourages believers to live out their faith with confidence and perseverance, continually growing in grace and knowledge of the Lord Jesus Christ.

APPENDIX F: No Once Saved, Always Saved: Upholding Scriptural Truth

Debunking the Concept of Eternal Security

The concept of 'Once Saved, Always Saved,' often associated with Calvinistic theology, posits that once a person is truly saved, they cannot lose their salvation. However, a thorough examination of Biblical teachings presents a different narrative, one that acknowledges the possibility of falling away from faith and the necessity of continual perseverance in the Christian journey.

The Fallacy of 'Once Saved, Always Saved'

1. **Calvinistic Interpretation of Perseverance**: Calvinism holds that those who are truly regenerated will persevere in faith. However, when a long-standing Christian abandons their faith, the Calvinistic response often is that the individual was never truly saved, suggesting a tautological reasoning that reinforces the 'Once Saved, Always Saved' doctrine.

2. **Scriptural Warnings Against Apostasy**: The Bible contains numerous warnings about the possibility of falling away. Hebrews 6:4-6, for example, speaks of those who have once been enlightened and tasted the heavenly gift, and yet fall away, making it impossible to be brought back to repentance.

3. **The Parable of the Sower (Matthew 13:1-23)**: This parable illustrates that the seed (the word of the kingdom) can be received but later abandoned due to various reasons, indicating the possibility of losing one's faith.

The Dynamic Nature of Faith

1. **Faith as a Continual Process**: Faith in the Christian life is not a one-time event but a dynamic, ongoing process. It requires constant nurturing through prayer, reading of Scripture, and community with other believers.

2. **The Role of Free Will**: Free will plays a crucial role in the Christian faith. While God extends His grace to humanity, individuals have the freedom to accept or reject this grace. The possibility of

choosing to turn away from God underscores the importance of free will in the doctrine of salvation.

Biblical Examples of Falling Away and Restoration

1. **King Saul (1 Samuel 15)**: Anointed by God, Saul later disobeyed God and was rejected as king, demonstrating that initial anointing or salvation can be lost due to disobedience and rebellion.

2. **Judas Iscariot (Matthew 26:14-16, 47-50; 27:3-5)**: As one of the twelve disciples, Judas's betrayal of Christ is a potent example of one who was part of Christ's inner circle but ultimately fell away.

3. **Simon Peter's Denial (Luke 22:54-62)**: Peter's denial of Christ, followed by his repentance and restoration, shows that while believers can falter, restoration is possible through repentance.

Theological Implications

1. **Assurance vs. Presumption**: There is a distinction between the assurance of salvation, which is grounded in faith and God's promises, and the presumption of eternal security, which can lead to complacency in one's spiritual life.

2. **The Necessity of Perseverance**: The doctrine of salvation encourages believers to persevere in their faith. This perseverance is not in their own strength but through the grace and power of the Holy Spirit.

3. **The Role of Community in Perseverance**: The Christian community plays a vital role in encouraging and supporting each other in the faith,

helping to prevent apostasy and promote perseverance.

The concept of 'Once Saved, Always Saved' oversimplifies the complex nature of salvation and faith. The Biblical narrative presents a more nuanced view, one that recognizes the real possibility of apostasy, the need for ongoing perseverance in faith, and the dynamic relationship between God's grace and human response. This understanding calls for a vigilant and active faith, nurtured continually through spiritual disciplines and community, and grounded in the hope and promises of God.

Scriptural Warnings Against Apostasy and Complacency

The doctrine of "Once Saved, Always Saved" posits that once a person is saved, they cannot lose their salvation under any circumstances. However, this concept is challenged by numerous scriptural passages that warn against apostasy and complacency in the Christian life. These warnings underscore the need for continual faith, vigilance, and obedience in the journey of salvation.

Understanding Apostasy

1. **Definition and Nature**: Apostasy refers to the act of abandoning or renouncing one's faith or religious beliefs. In the Christian context, it involves turning away from a genuine commitment to Christ and His teachings.

2. **Scriptural Examples**: The Bible contains several examples of individuals who turned away from their faith. For instance, Demas, mentioned in 2 Timothy 4:10, is noted for having loved this present

world and deserted Paul, indicating a departure from his earlier commitment.

Biblical Warnings

1. **Hebrews 6:4-6**: This passage warns of the impossibility of restoring those who have once been enlightened and then have fallen away. It suggests a real possibility of believers turning away from their faith.

2. **Matthew 24:10-13**: Jesus warned that many would fall away and betray one another in the end times, emphasizing the need for endurance in faith to be saved.

3. **2 Peter 2:20-22**: Peter describes the dire state of those who, after knowing the way of righteousness, turn back to their old sins, likening it to a dog returning to its vomit.

4. **Revelation 2-3**: The letters to the seven churches in Revelation contain warnings against losing their first love, complacency, and apostasy, calling for repentance and renewed commitment.

Theological Implications

1. **Free Will and Human Responsibility**: These warnings underscore the role of human free will in the salvation process. They suggest that believers must actively choose to remain faithful to Christ.

2. **The Nature of True Faith**: True faith is dynamic and involves a continual, active relationship with Christ. It is not merely a one-time event but a lifelong journey of faithfulness and obedience.

3. **Assurance of Salvation**: While believers can have assurance in Christ, this assurance does not negate the need for vigilance and perseverance in faith. Assurance should lead to a deeper commitment, not complacency.

4. **The Role of the Church**: The church is called to exhort and encourage believers to persevere in faith, offering support, teaching, and accountability to prevent apostasy.

Balancing Assurance with Diligence

1. **Eternal Security vs. Conditional Security**: The concept of eternal security needs to be balanced with the scriptural teachings on the conditional nature of salvation. Believers are secure in Christ, yet they are called to live out their faith actively.

2. **Perseverance of the Saints**: Perseverance involves continued faith, repentance, and obedience. It is the evidence of genuine salvation and the work of the Holy Spirit in the believer's life.

3. **Encouragement and Warning**: The scriptural warnings serve both as an encouragement to genuine believers and a warning to those who may be complacent or deceitful in their profession of faith.

The scriptural evidence suggests that the concept of "Once Saved, Always Saved" oversimplifies the complex nature of salvation and faith. The Biblical narrative presents a more nuanced view, recognizing the real possibility of apostasy, the necessity of ongoing faithfulness, and the dynamic relationship between God's grace and human response. This understanding calls for a vigilant and active faith, nurtured continually through spiritual disciplines, community support, and a deepening relationship with Christ.

The Necessity of Enduring Faith and Ongoing Repentance

In Christian theology, the concepts of enduring faith and ongoing repentance are crucial to understanding the nature of salvation. Contrary to the doctrine of "Once Saved, Always Saved," which is prevalent in some Calvinist circles, the Bible emphasizes the need for continuous faith and repentance throughout the Christian's life. This appendix explores the scriptural foundation for this view, affirming that salvation is not a one-time event but a dynamic journey requiring active participation and perseverance.

The Biblical Foundation of Enduring Faith

1. **Endurance in Faith**: Matthew 24:13 states, "But the one who endures to the end will be saved." This passage highlights the necessity of perseverance in faith as an ongoing process rather than a completed event.

2. **Parable of the Sower (Matthew 13:1-23)**: This parable illustrates different responses to the Gospel, showing that initial belief can be abandoned due to various trials or worldly distractions.

3. **Warnings in Hebrews**: The book of Hebrews is replete with exhortations to hold fast to faith (Hebrews 3:14, 4:11, 10:23-25). These passages

underscore the importance of remaining steadfast in faith to ensure participation in Christ's salvation.

4. **The Nature of Faith**: Faith in the New Testament is portrayed as active and living (James 2:26). It involves a continuous trust in and reliance upon God, not merely an initial act of belief.

Ongoing Repentance as a Key Aspect of Salvation

1. **Definition of Repentance**: Repentance in the Christian context involves a genuine change of mind and heart regarding sin, leading to a change in action and lifestyle.

2. **Jesus' Teaching on Repentance**: Jesus began His ministry with the call to repentance (Mark 1:15). This call is not limited to the initial act of turning to God but is an ongoing process throughout a Christian's life.

3. **Apostolic Exhortations**: The apostles continually exhorted believers to repentance. Acts 2:38, for instance, calls for repentance as a response to the Gospel, a theme reiterated throughout the New Testament.

4. **The Prodigal Son (Luke 15:11-32)**: This parable exemplifies the nature of repentance – a turning away from sin and a return to the father, symbolizing God's readiness to accept those who genuinely repent.

The Interplay of Assurance and Vigilance

1. **Assurance of Salvation**: Christians can have assurance of their salvation based on the promises of God and the witness of the Holy Spirit (Romans 8:16). However, this assurance does not negate the need for perseverance.

2. **Vigilance Against Complacency**: The New Testament warns against complacency and the assumption of security while living in disobedience (1 Corinthians 10:12, Revelation 3:1-3). Vigilance and spiritual alertness are key to maintaining one's faith.

Theological Implications

1. **Free Will and God's Sovereignty**: The necessity of enduring faith and ongoing repentance aligns with the concept of free will, acknowledging human responsibility in the process of salvation while affirming God's sovereignty.

2. **The Role of Community in Perseverance**: The Christian community plays a vital role in encouraging and exhorting one another to continue in faith and repentance (Hebrews 10:24-25).

3. **The Danger of Apostasy**: The possibility of falling away from faith (apostasy) is a real concern in the New Testament, urging believers to remain steadfast in their commitment to Christ.

The scriptural narrative presents a clear picture of the necessity of enduring faith and ongoing repentance for the Christian. Salvation is not merely a past event but involves a continual process of trusting in and turning to God. This dynamic understanding of salvation encourages believers to actively cultivate their relationship with God, relying on His grace and strength for perseverance and growth in the Christian life.

The Dangers of Presumptive Assurance in Christian Doctrine

The doctrine of "Once Saved, Always Saved," asserting that a person's salvation is secure regardless of their subsequent actions or faithfulness, presents significant theological and practical concerns within Christian doctrine. This concept, often equated with the Calvinistic understanding of perseverance, suggests that once salvation is attained, it cannot be forfeited. However, a thorough examination of scriptural teachings reveals that this presumption of assurance can lead to spiritual complacency and a misunderstanding of the nature of salvation.

Scriptural Foundations Challenging Presumptive Assurance

1. **Parable of the Sower (Matthew 13:1-23)**: This parable shows that the seed of the word of God can fall on different types of soil. The seed that falls on rocky ground or among thorns illustrates those who initially receive the word with joy but, due to trials or worldly concerns, fall away.

2. **Hebrews 6:4-6**: This passage warns against the danger of falling away after having received the knowledge of the truth. It suggests the real possibility that those who have once been enlightened can turn away from their faith.

3. **2 Peter 2:20-22**: Peter warns about the dire state of those who, after escaping the defilements of the world through the knowledge of Christ, become entangled in them again, stating that their latter state is worse than the first.

4. **Revelation 2-3**: The letters to the seven churches contain admonitions against losing fervor, compromising faith, and calls to repentance, indicating that perseverance in faith is crucial.

Theological Concerns with "Once Saved, Always Saved"

1. **Undermining the Call to Holiness**: This doctrine can diminish the Biblical call to holiness and continuous growth in faith. The New Testament is replete with exhortations to live a life worthy of the calling (Ephesians 4:1), suggesting that ongoing moral and spiritual vigilance is necessary.

2. **The Nature of Faith and Salvation**: Faith in the Biblical sense is dynamic and relational. It involves an ongoing trust and obedience to God. Salvation is not merely a legal transaction but encompasses a transformative relationship with Christ.

3. **Neglect of Apostolic Warnings**: The New Testament contains several warnings about the possibility of falling away, which are neglected or reinterpreted in the framework of "Once Saved, Always Saved." These warnings serve a purpose in encouraging believers to remain steadfast.

4. **Misinterpretation of Assurance**: Assurance of salvation in the New Testament is not an unconditional guarantee regardless of one's lifestyle

or faithfulness. Rather, it is a confident hope based on faith in Christ and evidenced by a life of obedience and fruitfulness.

Practical Implications of This Doctrine

1. **Complacency in Christian Life**: There's a danger that believers might become complacent, thinking that their salvation is secure regardless of their actions or spiritual state.

2. **Impact on Evangelism and Discipleship**: This belief can affect the church's mission, potentially leading to a lack of urgency in evangelism and a diminished focus on discipleship and spiritual growth.

3. **Challenges in Pastoral Care**: Addressing sin and encouraging repentance become complicated if individuals are assured of their salvation irrespective of their actions.

Balancing Assurance with Responsibility

1. **Biblical Assurance**: True Biblical assurance is grounded in a living faith and evidenced by a life transformed by the Holy Spirit. It involves both trust in God's promises and a response of obedience and faithfulness.

2. **Role of the Holy Spirit**: The Holy Spirit plays a crucial role in convicting believers of sin, guiding them in truth, and empowering them for holy living. This ongoing work is essential for persevering in faith.

3. **Continual Repentance and Faith**: The Christian life is marked by continual repentance and faith. Believers are called to daily take up their cross and follow Christ (Luke 9:23), indicating a need for ongoing spiritual vigilance.

The concept of "Once Saved, Always Saved" presents a theologically and practically flawed understanding of salvation. Biblical teachings emphasize the necessity of enduring faith, continual repentance, and obedience. Salvation is a dynamic process involving God's grace and human response. The Christian life is a journey of faithfulness and growth, marked by a balance of assurance in God's promises and responsibility to live according to His will.

Fostering a Balanced Understanding of Salvation and Perseverance

In the realm of Christian theology, the understanding of salvation and perseverance is a subject of vital importance. The doctrine often summarized as "Once Saved, Always Saved" suggests that once an individual attains salvation, it is impossible to lose it under any circumstances. However, this perspective requires careful scrutiny in light of scriptural teachings that emphasize the dynamic nature of faith, the need for ongoing perseverance, and the potential for apostasy. This comprehensive exploration seeks to foster a balanced understanding of salvation and perseverance, grounded in a thorough analysis of Biblical scripture.

Scriptural Foundations of Salvation

1. **Nature of Salvation**: Salvation in Christian theology is multifaceted. It is initiated by God's grace through faith in Jesus Christ (Ephesians 2:8-9) and involves a transformative process that includes justification, sanctification, and ultimately glorification (Romans 8:30).

2. **Role of Faith**: Faith is more than a one-time act; it is a sustained trust in and commitment to Jesus Christ. Faith is meant to grow and be nurtured throughout the believer's life (2 Thessalonians 1:3).

3. **Evidence of a Living Faith**: True faith is evidenced by good works and a transformed life (James 2:17, 26). These works are not the cause of salvation but are its fruit and proof.

The Necessity of Perseverance

1. **Enduring to the End**: Jesus' teachings emphasize the need for endurance in faith. Matthew 24:13 states, "But the one who endures to the end will be saved," highlighting perseverance as essential.

2. **Warning Against Apostasy**: The New Testament contains stark warnings about the danger of falling away. Hebrews 6:4-6, for example, speaks of those who have experienced the gifts of salvation and then fall away, emphasizing that restoration is impossible under such circumstances.

3. **The Parables of Jesus**: Many of Jesus' parables, such as the Parable of the Sower (Matthew 13:1-23), warn about the risks of a superficial or

temporary faith that does not endure in the face of trials or temptations.

Challenging Presumptive Assurance

1. **Misinterpretation of Eternal Security**: The doctrine of eternal security, when misconstrued as unconditional assurance irrespective of one's life and choices, can lead to complacency and a false sense of security.

2. **The Call to Ongoing Repentance**: Scripture repeatedly calls for repentance – a turning away from sin and turning towards God – which is a continuous process in the Christian life (Acts 3:19).

3. **Balancing Assurance and Vigilance**: While believers can and should have assurance of their salvation (1 John 5:13), this assurance is balanced with a call to vigilance and spiritual growth (2 Peter 1:5-10).

Theological and Practical Implications

1. **The Dynamic Relationship with God**: Salvation is not a static state but involves an ongoing, dynamic relationship with God, nurtured through prayer, scripture reading, and active involvement in the community of faith.

2. **Addressing Backsliding and Restoration**: The possibility of backsliding, or falling away from active faith, is acknowledged in scripture, yet there is also provision for restoration through repentance (1 John 1:9).

3. **Role of the Christian Community**: The Christian community plays a vital role in encouraging and supporting each member's faith and perseverance. This community is essential for accountability, growth, and mutual encouragement (Hebrews 10:24-25).

Conclusion

In conclusion, a balanced understanding of salvation and perseverance in the Christian life recognizes both the assurance of salvation through faith in Christ and the necessity of a living, active faith that endures through trials and temptations. This perspective upholds the Biblical call to vigilance and ongoing spiritual growth, acknowledging the potential for apostasy while also offering hope and means for restoration. It encourages believers to continually nurture their relationship with God, relying on His grace and the support of the Christian community to persevere in their faith journey.

APPENDIX G The Legacy of Calvinism After 560 Years

The Foundational Influence of John Calvin

Jean Cauvin's Beginnings and the Institutes

Jean Cauvin, better known as John Calvin, was a pivotal figure in the Protestant Reformation. Born in 1509 in France, he encountered Protestant teachings during his education. Facing religious persecution in Paris in 1534, Calvin relocated to Basel, Switzerland. Here, he penned "Institutes of the Christian Religion," a work synthesizing the thoughts of early church fathers, medieval theologians, and contemporary Reformers like Luther and Zwingli. This publication would eventually become the cornerstone for all Reformed churches in Europe and America.

Calvin's Theological Views

Calvin's theology centered on God's absolute sovereignty and the sinfulness of fallen humanity. He firmly believed that salvation was solely dependent on God's will, not human merit. This belief underpinned his doctrine of predestination, where God, by an eternal and unchangeable decision, determined who would be saved and who would be condemned. Calvin's theology was marked by its strictness and an emphasis on living a holy and virtuous life, free from pleasure and frivolity.

Implementing Calvinism in Geneva

In Geneva, Calvin, alongside William Farel, aimed to create a "city of God," a theocratic society where church and state functions merged. This led to the implementation of rigorous regulations governing various aspects of life, from religious practices to public morals. The enforcement of these rules was strict, often leading to harsh punishments for those who deviated from Calvinist doctrine.

The Controversial Execution of Michael Servetus

A notable incident during Calvin's reign in Geneva was the execution of Michael Servetus, a Spaniard who rejected the doctrine of the Trinity. Servetus was condemned by both Catholics and Calvinists but ultimately met his end at the hands of the latter. Calvin defended this act, arguing for the necessity of defending true Christian doctrine, even to the point of shedding blood.

Calvinism's Spread and Influence

After Calvin's death in 1564, his version of reform continued to influence many regions. Protestant reformers from different countries, inspired by Calvinist teachings, began reform movements in their homelands. Calvinism spread to France, the Netherlands, Scotland, England, and later to North America with the Puritans. This widespread influence arguably made Calvin more impactful in shaping the Protestant Reformation than Martin Luther.

500 Years of Calvinism: A Retrospective

Today, half a millennium since Calvin's birth, his teachings continue to resonate in various Protestant denominations. The World Alliance of Reformed Churches, as of the last report, had 75 million adherents in over 100 countries. Calvinism, in its various forms, remains a significant force in global Christianity.

Critiquing Calvinism from a Biblical Perspective

Predestination and Free Will

The doctrine of predestination, a hallmark of Calvinism, raises significant theological and ethical concerns. It suggests that God's grace is selectively bestowed, challenging the concept of a loving and just God who desires all to be saved (1 Timothy 2:4). This doctrine contradicts the biblical portrayal of human free will and the call for all to seek salvation. More on this below.

Theocracy and Religious Freedom

Calvin's attempt to create a theocratic state in Geneva presents a problematic fusion of church and state powers. This blending often led to the suppression of religious freedom and harsh punishments for those with differing beliefs. Such an approach seems at odds with the New Testament teachings that emphasize spiritual governance rather than earthly political dominion (John 18:36).

The Execution of Michael Servetus

The execution of Michael Servetus under Calvin's watch is a stark example of religious intolerance and extremism. This act, defended by Calvin, contradicts the Christian call to love one's enemies and to practice forgiveness and tolerance (Matthew 5:44). It reflects a departure from the compassionate and forgiving nature of Jesus Christ's ministry.

Legacy and Modern Interpretations

While Calvinism has significantly shaped Protestantism, its rigid doctrines have also been a source of division and controversy. Modern interpretations of Calvinism often attempt to reconcile its harsher aspects with a more inclusive and compassionate Christian theology. However, the historical legacy of Calvinism, with its emphasis on predestination and theocratic rule, continues to pose challenges for contemporary Christian thought and practice.

Assessing Calvin's Impact on Geneva and Beyond

Calvin's Transformative Influence on Geneva

Moral Reformation in Geneva

John Calvin, a central figure in the Protestant Reformation, exerted a profound influence on the city of Geneva. Described by the Encyclopedia of Religion, Calvin transformed Geneva from a morally lax city into one governed by a stringent moral code. This shift wasn't just spiritual but also had a tangible impact on the daily lives of Geneva's citizens.

Economic and Cultural Revitalization

Dr. Sabine Witt of Berlin's German Historical Museum points out another significant change: the influx of Protestant refugees, particularly the Huguenots, dramatically increased Geneva's population and invigorated its economy. These refugees brought with them a strong work ethic, akin to Calvin's, significantly boosting the city's economic activities, particularly in printing and timepiece manufacturing.

The Impact of Calvinist Refugees

Geneva as a Refuge for Protestants

Geneva became a sanctuary for persecuted Protestants from various regions, including England, under the Catholic Queen Mary I. These refugees contributed to the development of a unique Calvinist theology, described by the religious journal *Christ in der Gegenwart* as "the theology of the persecuted." This period also saw the publication of the Geneva Bible in 1560, a significant milestone as it was the first English Bible with numbered verses and was compact enough to encourage personal Bible study. This Bible would later accompany the Puritans to North America in 1620.

Geneva's Darker Side Under Calvin

The Execution of Michael Servetus

Despite being a refuge for many, Geneva under Calvin was not a haven for all. The case of Michael Servetus, a scholar who challenged the doctrine of the Trinity, is particularly notable. Servetus fled persecution in France, only to be arrested, tried for heresy, and executed in Geneva in 1553. This event, as historian Friedrich Oehninger notes, remains a blight on Calvin's otherwise impactful legacy.

Calvin's Prodigious Output and Authoritarian Rule

Calvin's Extensive Works and Sermons

Calvin was remarkably prolific in his writings and preaching. His literary legacy includes over 100 reference works, 1,000 letters, and approximately 4,000 sermons delivered in Geneva. Through these works, Calvin not only shared his vision of Christianity but also sought to dictate the conduct of Christian life, particularly in Geneva.

Envisioning Geneva as a 'City of God'

Calvin's vision for Geneva was that of a 'city of God,' a place where Christian virtues and values were not just preached but enforced. This approach to governance intertwined religious belief with civic regulation, reflecting Calvin's view of a society governed by divine principles.

The Lasting Impact of Calvin's Reforms

Diminished Influence in Modern Geneva

Reflecting on the enduring influence of Calvin's reforms, the Swiss Federal Statistics Office reported in 2000 that only 16% of Geneva's inhabitants identified with the Reformed (Calvinist) Church. Interestingly, there are now more Catholics than Calvinists in Geneva. This statistic points to a significant shift away from the religious landscape shaped by Calvin in the 16th century.

Calvin's theological contributions and extensive writings have left an indelible mark on Protestant Christianity. However, the waning adherence to Calvinism in modern Geneva suggests a shift in religious dynamics and the evolution of societal values since Calvin's era. This decline in Calvinist influence in Geneva invites reflection on the nature of religious reform and the complex legacy of influential religious figures like John Calvin.

Exploring the Complex Landscape of Post-Reformation Religious Disunity

The Fragmentation of Christendom in Post-Reformation Europe

Diverse Allegiances and Theological Rifts

Following the Reformation, Europe became a mosaic of religious allegiances, with regions and cities aligning with

Catholicism, Lutheranism, or Calvinism. This period marked a significant departure from the previously unified religious landscape dominated by the Catholic Church. Despite a common criticism of Catholic doctrines, Protestant Reformers found themselves in disagreement on several theological matters.

The Core Issue: Interpretations of Scripture and Sacraments

Disagreements on Scriptural Interpretation

All Protestant factions agreed on the primacy of the Bible in Christian faith, but this consensus was superficial. Deep divisions emerged regarding the interpretation of key scriptural passages and doctrines. One of the central issues of contention was the understanding of the Last Supper and Christ's presence in the Eucharist.

Diverging Views on the Eucharist

The interpretation of the Eucharist became a major point of division among the Reformers. Different groups within the Protestant movement developed their own understanding of Christ's presence during the Last Supper, leading to varied and sometimes conflicting sacramental practices.

The Controversial Doctrine of Predestination in Calvinism

Development of Predestination

One of the most contentious doctrines to emerge in this era was the Calvinist concept of predestination. This doctrine, developed over time within Calvinism, proposed that God had predetermined the salvation or damnation of individuals.

Debates Over Predestination's Nature

The doctrine of predestination was not monolithic within Calvinism; it sparked intense debate and division. One group of Calvinists asserted that God, prior to the fall of man, had predestined only a select few for salvation through Christ, leaving the rest to their fate. This interpretation implied a lack of equality among humans in the eyes of God.

Alternative Views on Salvation and Free Will

In contrast, another faction within Calvinism believed that salvation was accessible to all humanity. According to this view, individuals had the free will to accept or reject salvation, thereby placing the responsibility of salvation on human choice rather than divine decree.

Understanding Simple Foreknowledge and Human Freedom

The Concept of Simple Foreknowledge in Theology

Defining Simple Foreknowledge

Simple Foreknowledge is a theological concept that posits God's omniscience, particularly His knowledge of future events, without implying that this knowledge causally determines these events. This view maintains that God's foreknowledge is comprehensive, encompassing all future contingencies and outcomes.

The Compatibility of Divine Foreknowledge and Human Freedom

Harmonizing Foreknowledge with Human Choice

Advocates of Simple Foreknowledge argue that God's omniscience is compatible with human freedom. They assert that while God foreknows every decision and event, His foreknowledge does not influence or dictate human choices. This perspective maintains that human beings possess genuine free will, making decisions that are not predetermined by divine knowledge.

The Logical Sequence of Foreknowledge

In this framework, the sequence of events and God's foreknowledge is logically structured. An event is logically prior to God's foreknowledge, meaning that God knows an event because it will happen, not the other way around. Although God's foreknowledge is chronologically prior to the event, it is the event itself that determines what God foreknows.

Illustrating Simple Foreknowledge

The Shadow Analogy

A helpful analogy for understanding Simple Foreknowledge is the concept of a shadow foreshadowing a person's arrival. Just as seeing a shadow indicates that a person is about to come around the corner, without the shadow causing the person's arrival, so too does God's foreknowledge act as a preview of future events. The shadow does not determine the person's actions; rather, the person's presence and actions create the shadow.

The Infallible Barometer Analogy

Another illustration of Simple Foreknowledge is likened to an infallible barometer predicting weather. The barometer's readings are always accurate, reflecting the future state of the weather. However, the barometer does not influence the weather conditions; it merely indicates what they will be. Similarly, God's foreknowledge is akin to an infallible indicator of future events. It reveals what will occur without dictating or constraining these occurrences.

Implications of Simple Foreknowledge on Divine Omniscience and Human Agency

Preserving Human Free Will

One of the key implications of Simple Foreknowledge is the preservation of human free will. Under this view, human beings are free moral agents, capable of making choices independently of divine predestination or foreordained plans. God's knowledge of future events does not impinge upon the freedom of these events to unfold according to the decisions of free moral agents.

The Nature of God's Omniscience

Simple Foreknowledge also sheds light on the nature of God's omniscience. It posits a God who is all-knowing, yet His knowledge does not interfere with the course of human history. God's omniscience is seen as a perfect understanding of all possible outcomes, rather than a determinant of those outcomes.

Theological Significance and Debates Surrounding Simple Foreknowledge

Addressing Predestination and Free Will

The concept of Simple Foreknowledge is particularly significant in theological discussions about predestination and free will. It offers a perspective that upholds the sovereignty and omniscience of God while simultaneously affirming the autonomy and responsibility of human beings in their moral and spiritual decisions.

Debates and Challenges

Despite its appeal, Simple Foreknowledge is not without its critics and challenges. Some theologians argue that if God foreknows every choice and action, it might still imply a form of determinism, even if not directly causal. Others question how God's foreknowledge and human free will can coexist without some level of conflict or contradiction.

Concluding Reflections on Simple Foreknowledge

The concept of Simple Foreknowledge presents a compelling framework for understanding the relationship between divine omniscience and human freedom. By positing that God's foreknowledge is indicative rather than determinative, this perspective allows for a harmonious coexistence of God's all-knowing nature and human free will. The analogies of the shadow and the infallible barometer effectively illustrate how God's foreknowledge can be understood as a perfect awareness of future events that does not compromise human agency or the unfolding of history.

In essence, Simple Foreknowledge offers a nuanced approach to some of the most profound theological questions regarding the nature of God and the autonomy of human beings. It acknowledges the complexity of these issues and provides a framework that respects both the majesty of divine knowledge and the dignity of human choice. As with all theological concepts, it invites ongoing reflection and discussion, encouraging believers to delve deeper into the mysteries of faith, divine foreknowledge, and human freedom.

The Ongoing Struggle Within Calvinism

Post-Calvin Debates on Divine Sovereignty and Human Agency

Long after Calvin's death, his followers continued to grapple with these theological issues. The debates centered around reconciling the concept of God's sovereign decree with the notion of human free will and the equal opportunity for salvation among all people.

Implications of These Debates

These internal debates within Calvinism had significant implications. They not only shaped the theological landscape of Calvinism itself but also influenced its interactions with other Protestant denominations and the Catholic Church. The disagreements highlighted the complexities inherent in attempting to understand and articulate the nature of divine providence and human responsibility in the context of salvation.

Edward D. Andrews

Concluding Thoughts on Religious Disunity Post-Reformation

The era following the Reformation was marked by a proliferation of religious disunity, as evidenced by the divergent paths taken by various Protestant groups. The debates within Calvinism over predestination and free will exemplify the broader challenges faced by the Reformers in their efforts to define Christian doctrine based on their interpretations of Scripture.

This period of religious fragmentation reflects the difficulties inherent in reconciling differing theological perspectives, particularly concerning such profound mysteries as divine sovereignty and human free will. The ongoing debates and divisions underscore the complexity of theological discourse and the enduring impact of these discussions on the shape of Christian belief and practice.

In sum, the post-Reformation era was not only a time of breaking away from Catholic orthodoxy but also a period of intense internal struggle within Protestantism itself. The divergent views on predestination within Calvinism serve as a microcosm of the broader theological and ecclesiastical challenges faced by a Christendom grappling with new freedoms and responsibilities in interpreting Scripture and defining the Christian faith.

Calvinism's Complex and Troubled Legacy

Calvinism and Its Role in Historical Injustices

The Dutch Reformed Church and Apartheid

In the 20th century, a disturbing chapter in Calvinism's history unfolded with the Dutch Reformed Church in South Africa. This church, influenced by Calvinist theology, used the doctrine of predestination to justify racial discrimination, particularly during the apartheid era. They propagated the notion that Afrikaners were God's chosen people, while black South Africans were deemed an inferior race. This theological stance provided religious justification for the government's policy of white supremacy, as highlighted by Nelson Mandela, South Africa's first black president.

Acknowledgment and Apology for Supporting Apartheid

The Rustenburg Declaration

In the 1990s, the Dutch Reformed Church publicly acknowledged its grievous error in supporting apartheid. Through the Rustenburg Declaration, church leaders admitted to misusing the Bible to endorse apartheid, inadvertently attributing divine sanction to these racial policies. This confession was a significant step in addressing the church's role in perpetuating racial prejudice and suffering under the guise of religious doctrine.

Reflecting on John Calvin's Personal Legacy and Influence

John Calvin's Death and Self-Reflection

John Calvin passed away in Geneva in 1564. At his deathbed, he expressed gratitude for the honors bestowed upon him, despite feeling undeserving, and sought forgiveness for his personal failings, particularly his struggles with impatience and anger. This moment of self-awareness and humility offers a glimpse into Calvin's complex character.

The Protestant Work Ethic and Calvin's Influence

Calvin's influence extended beyond theology into the realm of cultural and ethical values. The Protestant work ethic, characterized by qualities such as industriousness, self-discipline, and dedication to duty, bears a strong resemblance to Calvin's personal values and teachings. This ethic became a defining feature of Protestant communities and had a lasting impact on various aspects of societal development.

The Enduring Impact and Challenges of Calvinism

Calvinism's Mixed Legacy

Calvinism, through its history, has left a mixed legacy. On one hand, it has been a driving force behind significant cultural and ethical developments. On the other, it has been implicated in historical injustices, as seen in its role in apartheid South Africa.

The Need for Ongoing Reflection and Reformation

The history of Calvinism, particularly its involvement in apartheid, necessitates ongoing reflection and reformation within the church. It highlights the importance of critically examining theological doctrines and their real-world implications, ensuring they align with the core Christian principles of love, justice, and equality.

Learning from History

The public apology of the Dutch Reformed Church for its role in apartheid is a vital step in acknowledging past wrongs and seeking to rectify them. It serves as a reminder of the church's responsibility to uphold justice and resist the misuse of theological doctrines for oppressive purposes.

Calvin's Personal Reflections at Life's End

Calvin's expressions of humility and recognition of his personal shortcomings at the end of his life offer an important lesson in self-reflection and the acknowledgment of human fallibility. It underscores the need for leaders, religious or otherwise, to remain humble and open to introspection and growth.

Conclusions on Calvinism's Legacy

Reflecting on 500 years of Calvinism, it's evident that John Calvin's influence on Christianity has been profound and far-reaching. However, from a biblical perspective, certain aspects of Calvinism, such as its predestinarian theology and theocratic tendencies, are at odds with a broader understanding of biblical teachings. The legacy of Calvinism, while significant, also serves as a reminder of the need for continual reformation and reflection within the Christian tradition, ensuring that the teachings and practices of the faith align with the core principles of love, grace, and freedom exemplified in the life and teachings of Jesus Christ.

While Calvin's efforts in Geneva produced significant changes in his time, the long-term impact of these reforms shows a nuanced picture. It's a legacy of both positive transformation and controversial actions, reflecting the complexities inherent in merging religious beliefs with civic governance. As we look back on Calvin's legacy, it's crucial to critically assess both the achievements and the shortcomings of his vision and its implementation in the ever-evolving landscape of religious thought and practice.

Concluding Reflections

John Calvin's efforts in Geneva were characterized by a mix of religious fervor, moral strictness, and a vision of societal transformation under the banner of Christianity. While his reforms led to the economic and cultural revitalization of Geneva, they also bore the marks of religious intolerance and authoritarian rule. The execution of Michael Servetus remains a particularly troubling aspect of this legacy.

In conclusion, Calvinism, as reflected in the actions of the Dutch Reformed Church during the apartheid era and in the life and teachings of John Calvin, presents a complex and multifaceted legacy. While it has contributed positively to cultural and ethical values, it has also been associated with significant historical injustices. The church's recognition of its past mistakes and Calvin's personal reflections remind us of the importance of humility, continuous self-examination, and the responsibility to ensure that religious teachings promote justice, equality, and the dignity of all people. This legacy invites a balanced and nuanced understanding of Calvinism, acknowledging both its contributions and its failings, and inspires a commitment to ensuring that faith serves as a force for good in the world.

Bibliography

Akin, D. L., Nelson, D. P., & Peter R. Schemm, J. (2007). *A Theology for the Church.* Nashville: B & H Publishing.

Anders, M., & McIntosh, D. (2009). *Holman Old Testament Commentary - Deuteronomy (pp. 359-360). .* Nashville: B&H Publishing.

Andrews, E. D. (2015). *EVIDENCE THAT YOU ARE TRULY CHRISTIAN: Keep Testing Yourselves to See If You Are In the Faith - Keep Examining Yourselves.* Cambridge, OH: Christian Publishing House.

Andrews, E. D. (2016). *INTERPRETING THE BIBLE: Introduction to Biblical Hermeneutics.* Cambridge, OH: Christian Publishing House.

Andrews, E. D. (2016). *YOUR GUIDE FOR DEFENDING THE BIBLE: Self-Education of the Bible Made Easy.* Cambridge, OH: Christian Publishing House.

Andrews, E. D. (2016). *YOUR WORD IS TRUTH: Being Sanctified In the Truth.* Cambridge, OH: Christian Publishing House.

Andrews, E. D. (2017). *HUMAN IMPERFECTION: While We Were Sinners Christ Died For Us.* Cambridge, OH: Christian Ppublishing House.

Andrews, E. D. (2018). *WHAT WILL HAPPEN IF YOU DIE?* Cambridge, OH: Christian Publishing House.

Andrews, E. D. (2018). *WHY ME?: When Bad Things Happen to Good People.* Cambridge, OH: Christian Publishing House.

Andrews, E. D. (2019). *SATAN: Know Your Enemy.* Cambridge, OH: Christian Publishing House.

Andrews, E. D. (2023). *CHRISTIAN APOLOGETICS: Answering the Tough Questions: Evidence and Reason in Defense of the Faith.* Cambridge, Ohio: Christian Publishing House.

Andrews, E. D. (2023). *JOHN CALVIN: A Solitary Quest for the Truth.* Cambridge, Ohio: Christian Publishing House.

Andrews, E. D. (2023). *LIFE DOES HAVE A PURPOSE: Discovering and Living Your Ultimate Purpose.* Cambridge, OH: Christian Publishing House.

Andrews, E. D. (2023). *MERE CHRISTIANITY REIMAGINED: Rediscovering the Faith for the 21st Century.* Cambridge, OH: Christian Publishing House.

Andrews, E. D. (2023). *UNSHAKABLE BELIEFS: Strategies for Strengthening and Defending Your Faith.* Cambridge, OH: Christian Publishing House.

Arnold, C. E. (2002). *Zondervan Illustrated Bible Backgrounds Commentary Volume 2: John, Acts.* . Grand Rapids, MI: Zondervan.

Arnold, C. E. (2002). *Zondervan Illustrated Bible Backgrounds Commentary Volume 3: Romans to Philemon.* Grand Rapids: Zondervan.

Arnold, C. E. (2002). *Zondervan Illustrated Bible Backgrounds Commentary Volume 4: Hebrews to Revelation.* Grand Rapids, MI: Zondervan.

Arnold, C. E. (2002). *Zondervan Illustrated Bible Backgrounds Commentary: Matthew, Mark, Luke, vol. 1.* Grand Rapids, MI: Zondervan.

Barker, K. L., & Bailey, W. (2001). *The New American Commentary: vol. 20, Micah, Nahum, Habakkuk, Zephaniah.* Nashville, TN: Broadman & Holman Publishers.

Bercot, D. W. (1998). *A Dictionary of Early Christian Beliefs.* Peabody: Hendrickson.

Boles, K. L. (1993). *The College Press NIV commentary: Galatians & Ephesians.* Joplin, MO: College Press.

Boyd, G. A., & Eddy, P. R. (2002, 2009). *Across the Spectrum [Secon Edition].* Grand Rapids: Baker Academic.

Brand, C., Draper, C., & Archie, E. (2003). *Holman Illustrated Bible Dictionary: Revised, Updated and Expanded.* Nashville, TN: Holman.

Bratcher, R. G., & Hatton, H. (1993). *A Handbook on the Revelation to John.* New York: United Bible Societies.

Bromiley, G. W., & Friedrich, G. (1964-). *Theological Dictionary of the New Testament, ed. Gerhard Kittel, vol. 4.* Grand Rapids, MI: Eerdmans.

Bullinger, E. W. (1898). *Figures of Speech Used in the Bible.* London; New York: E. & J. B. Young & Co.

Elwell, W. A. (2001). *Evangelical Dictionary of Theology (Second Edition).* Grand Rapids: Baker Academic.

Enns, P. P. (1997). *The Moody Handbook of Theology.* Chicago: Moody Press.

Erickson, M. J. (1998). *Christian Theology.* Grand Rapids, MI: Baker Academic.

Erickson, M. J. (2013). *Christian Theology (Third Edition).* Grand Rapids, MI: Baker Academic.

Ferguson, E. (2009). *Baptism in the Early Church: History, Theology, and Liturgy in the First Five Centuries .* Grand Rapids, MI: Eerdmans.

Friberg, T., Friberg, B., & Miller, N. F. (2000). *Analytical Lexicon of the Greek New Testament.* Grand Rapids: Baker Books.

Friberg, T., Friberg, B., & Miller, N. F. (2000). *Analytical Lexicon of the Greek New Testament, Baker's Greek New Testament Library.* Grand Rapids, MI: Baker Books.

Gangel, K. O. (1998). *Holman New Testament Commentary: Acts.* Nashville, TN: Broadman & Holman Publishers.

Gangel, K. O. (2000). *Holman New Testament Commentary, vol. 4, John .* Nashville, TN: Broadman & Holman Publishers.

Geisler, N. L. (2011). *Systematic Theology in One Volume.* Minneapolis, MN: Bethany House.

Grudem, W. (2011). *Making Sense of the Bible: One of Seven Parts from Grudem's Systematic Theology (Making Sense of Series).* Grand Rapids: Zondervan.

Gruden, W. (2011). *Are Miraculous Gifts for Today?: 4 Views (Counterpoints: Bible and Theology).* Grand Rapids: Zondervan.

Harris, R. L., Archer, G. L., & Waltke, B. K. (1999, c1980). *Theological Wordbook of the Old Testament.* Chicago: Moody Press.

Hill, J. (2006). *Zondervan Handbook to the History of Christianity.* Oxford: Lion.

Keener, C. S. (1993). *The IVP Bible Background Commentary: New Testament.* Downer Groves, IL: InterVarsity Press.

Kittel, G., Friedrich, G., & Bromiley, G. W. (1995, c1985). *Theological Dictionary of the New Testament.* Grand Rapids: Eerdmans.

Knight, G. W. (1992). *The Pastoral Epistles: A Commentary on the Greek Text, New International Greek Testament Commentary.*

Grand Rapids, MI; Carlisle, England: W.B. Eerdmans; Paternoster Press.

Larson, K. (2000). *Holman New Testament Commentary, vol. 9, I & II Thessalonians, I & II Timothy, Titus, Philemon.* Nashville, TN: Broadman & Holman Publishers.

Lea, T. D. (1999). *Holman New Testament Commentary: Vol. 10, Hebrews, James.* Nashville, TN: Broadman & Holman Publishers.

McMinn, M. R. (2010). *Psychology, Theology, and Spirituality in Christian Counseling (AACC Library).* Carol Stream, IL: Tyndale House Publishers.

McReynolds, P. R. (1999). *Word Study: Greek-English.* Carol Stream: Tyndale House Publishers.

Mounce, W. D. (2006). *Mounce's Complete Expository Dictionary of Old & New Testament Words.* Grand Rapids, MI: Zondervan.

Polhill, J. B. (2001). *The New American Commentary 26: Acts.* Nashville: Broadman & Holman Publishers.

Pratt Jr, R. L. (2000). *Holman New Testament Commentary: I & II Corinthians, vol. 7.* Nashville: Broadman & Holman Publishers.

Ramsey, B. (. (2006). *Manichean Debate (Works of Saint Augustine).* New City Press: Hyde Park.

Robertson, P. E. (Spring 1998). Theology of the Healthy Church. *The Theological Educator: A Journal of Theology and Ministry*, 45-52.

Stein, R. H. (1994). *A Basic Guide to Interpreting the Bible: Playing by the Rules.* Grand Rapids: Baker Books.

Swindoll, C. R., & Zuck, R. B. (2003). *Understanding Christian Theology.* Nashville, TN: Thomas Nelson Publishers.

Terry, M. S. (1883). *Biblical Hermeneutics: A Treatise on the Interpretation of the Old and New Testaments.* Grand Rapids: Zondervan.

Thomas, R. L. (1992). *Revelation 1-7: An Exegetical Commentary* . Chicago, IL: Moody Publishers.

Thomas, R. L. (1995). *Revelation 8-22: An Exegetical Commentary* . Chicago, IL: Moody Publishers.

Thomas, R. L. (1998, 1981). *New American Standard Hebrew-Aramaic and Greek Dictionaries: Updated Edition.* Anaheim: Foundation Publications, Inc.

Towns, E. L. (2002). *Theology for Today.* Belmont: Wadsworth Group.

Towns, E. L. (2006). *Concise Bible Dictrines: Clear, Simple, and Easy-to-Understand Explanations of Bible Doctrines.* Chattanooga: AMG Publishers.

Vine, W. E. (1996). *Vine's Expository Dictionary of Old and New Testament Words.* Nashville: Thomas Nelson.

Walls, D., & Anders, M. (1996). *Holman New Testament Commentary: I & II Peter, I, II & III John, Jude.* Nashville: Broadman & Holman Publishers.

Walton, J. H. (2009). *Zondervan Illustrated Bible Backgrounds Commentary (Old Testament) Volume 1: Genesis, Exodus, Leviticus, Numbers, Deuteronomy.* Grand Rapids, MI: Zondervan.

Walton, J. H. (2009). *Zondervan Illustrated Bible Backgrounds Commentary (Old Testament) Volume 3: 1 & 2 Kings, 1 & 2 Chronicles, Ezra, Nehemiah, Esthe.* Grand Rapids, MI: Zondervan.

Walton, J. H. (2009). *Zondervan Illustrated Bible Backgrounds Commentary (Old Testament) Volume 5: The Minor Prophets, Job, Psalms, Proverbs, Ecclesiastes, Song of Songs.* Grand Rapids, M: Zondervan.

Watson, R. (1832). *A Biblical and Theological Dictionary: Explanatory of the History, Manners and Customs of the Jews.* New York: Waugh and T. Mason.

Weber, S. K. (2000). *Holman New Testament Commentary, vol. 1, Matthew.* Nashville, TN: Broadman & Holman Publishers.

Zodhiates, S. (2000, c1992, c1993). *The Complete Word Study Dictionary: New Testament.* Chattanooga: AMG Publishers.

Zuck, R. B. (1991). *Basic Bible Interpretation: A Prafctical Guide to Discovering Biblical Truth.* Colorado Springs: David C. Cook.